From

From the Pit of Hell

A True Story

Steve Amos

paternoster
Lifestyle

08 07 06 05 04 03 02   7 6 5 4 3 2 1

Paternoster Lifestyle is an imprint of
Paternoster Publishing,
PO Box 300, Carlisle, Cumbria, CA3 0QS, UK
and Paternoster Publishing USA
PO Box 1047, Waynesboro, GA 30830-2047
www.paternoster-publishing.com

British Library Cataloguing in Publication Data

A catalogue record for this book is available from the
British Library

ISBN 1-85078-443-4

Cover design by Campsie
Printed in Great Britain by
Cox and Wyman, Reading, Berkshire, RG1 8EX

Dedication

This book is dedicated to my wife, Nanette,
and my boys, Freddie and Dudley;
And for my little girl Marie – wherever you
are;
And little Melissa, who's with Jesus now;
All my family who've loved me including
Black Nanny and Cockney Grandad Jim
(who's traded all the cares of this world, for
the glory of the next);
Mum and Dad, Pam, John and Linda;
Minty and Katie, Matt and Tina (and Tess!)
And the reader, whoever you are.

Contents

Acknowledgements

I would like to thank all my friends and ene-
mies – past and present – and those who have
made this book happen.

My lovely wife Nanette, who has loved me,
truly through thick and thin – and Freddie and
Dudley – my boys.

My Pastor Barry Minty for being a great
friend, as well as my father-in-law – and Chrisie
his wife – and everyone in my home church in
Newton Abbot.

Living Waters Pentecostal Church, Paignton,
for the consideration and care they showed me
when I first became a Christian.

My wonderful mum and dad (I love you so
much).

All the boys and girls in all the schools I have
ever been in (too many to name!).

Thank you to Jolyon Tuck for your integrity
and creativity and for all the time you spent
with me, and my lousy English!.

The Knights of Antioch Christian Motorcyclists
Club, and the Christian Motorcyclists Association.

Chris and Irene Rhodes – for your graciousness with me in your lovely home!

Pastor Stan and Doreen Hyde – 'you taught me so much, I couldn't begin to tell you how much I value your part in my life'.

Foreword

The first time I met Steve Amos was at a church named Living Waters in Torquay. I had gone to the church with my wife to talk about the love of God. I was greeted upon my arrival by a bunch of guys who would have looked more at home in a chapter of the Hells Angels than standing outside of a church welcoming people. These guys were The Knights of Antioch, a bunch of bikers who ride around towns spreading the word of God. They have a ministry that is unique and one that God uses mightily. Steve Amos was one of the riders. His story is a compelling read and tells of how Steve went to the gates of Hell and came back through the love of God. He lived a life in the fast lane and soon came crashing down. God was there to pick up the pieces. Steve is certainly a walking miracle showing what God can do in our lives if we let him. Going from violent drug addict, prisoner and a thief to a bike-riding, God-filled evangelist is nothing short of a miracle. God leaps from nearly every page in this book and we see that

no matter what depths we go to, God can help
us. It is my privilege to know Steve Amos.

                                    Bobby Ball

Introduction

Even today I find it a bizarre sensation to walk into a classroom and see thirty or so faces staring up at me expectantly, waiting for me to speak. It has been over seven years since I gave my first drugs awareness talk in a school, but that does not make the situation any less strange when I think back to the person I used to be. I arrive at the school on my motorbike, which always generates interest from the kids. They see a man dressed in leathers, with a close-shaven head and a goatee beard walk up to the main door of the school. Sometimes I feel eyebrows being raised in the staff room upon my entrance. But I expect people to take me as I am. I am there to do a job, and if the head teacher or governors thought I was incapable of doing the job then I would not be there.

When I walk into the classroom I know not to expect any respect. Respect must be earned, and so that is what I strive to do as soon as possible. Whilst the kids talk amongst themselves I make use of the blackboard. In this school the 'blackboard' is white, with pens in a selection of colours. I take the green pen and I draw a cannabis leaf. There are sniggers from my audience and I know that several have recognised the image. I hear muttering, the words 'pot' and 'dope' circulate and I know that I have their interest.

I turn around and introduce myself.

'All right everyone, my name is Steve Amos, and I'm here to talk to you about drug awareness.'

I have given talks in this school before, and so some of the kids have an idea what to expect of me. Having made a couple of light-hearted comments about my time in prison and my experience of guns, I have had the chance to assess my audience and identify where the more rebellious personalities are sitting. To me these children are not troublemakers, instead they are my tools. These louder students are the ones who will be honest and bring my talk to life. The laughter at these comments dies down as they realise that I am not joking. Although I appear flippant, I am deadly serious.

I return to the blackboard. I write 50p next to the cannabis leaf, then £250,000 in the middle of the board. Adjacent to this I draw a cross.

I then explain that I paid 50p for my first joint, that I have spent about £250,000 on drugs in my life, and that I have died. This raises a laugh, but again the laughter soon fades as they see the expression on my face. Drugs are no laughing matter. Now I have their full attention, I rattle off a list of drugs that I have taken, and then it is down to business.

From experience I know that these sessions work best when I answer questions from the floor. I am of the opinion that if the kids are to be aware about drugs then I should talk about what they want to know. At the same time I make it clear that, although they want to know about it, they would never want to do it. So I open the subject up to the 'audience'. It comes as no surprise to see just one hand raised with a question. The larger personalities have disappeared and I take a question from one of the quieter lads in the room.

'Can you talk about acid?' he asks.

Those sat around him pass comment under their breath; they never realised he was into that kind of thing. This makes him feel the need to justify his enquiry,

'I've heard there are lots of different sorts, and that they have different effects, some are okay, others are really dangerous.'

And so this is where I begin. I talk about the different types of LSD and explain that although there are various degrees of danger, the 'safest' form of acid is by no means safe.

The ice now broken, I am flooded with questions about my childhood, about glue-sniffing, about using needles, and about the sort of trips I had whilst on LSD.

As I talk about my life, I find myself relating my stories to scenes from films. In this one session alone, I have mentioned seven films to illustrate my various points.

'Have you seen the film Alien?'

A great 'Yes!' erupts from the class.

I smile and look across at their teacher, 'I wouldn't say that too loud with your teacher in the room. It's an 18 certificate and none of you can be over 16!'

And so, as I find what I'm saying becomes too heavy, I make a joke to lighten the atmosphere. I talk about the time a small cartoon banana followed me around for twelve hours when I was on acid; and balance this with the story of how my cousin, Morris, almost lost his arm by experimenting with the same drug. And so I have succeeded in gaining their attention, and also a certain degree of respect. As the bell rings for lunch, I am free to leave, but on this occasion, as I have found quite often, nobody leaves, and instead we carry on talking for another 20 minutes.

Before I actually go, I take one final question.

'Don't you miss the excitement of your life on drugs?'

I laugh at the thought of it.

'I did drugs to calm down mate!' I reply, 'Trust me when I say I'm much wilder now than I ever was then! Life today is much more exciting!'

As I leave, I hope they will have learnt something from what I have said, and I trust I will have made an impression on their young lives. And, as I think about where their lives will go from here, I think back to my own childhood. How it might have been different if I had had a Steve Amos come to my school and talk to me about the danger of drugs. And then, with regret, I smile to myself as it dawns on me that I probably wouldn't have been in school in the first place!

1

Gangs and Glue

I was born in Gravesend, Kent, on 6 July 1967. Brought up on the King's Farm estate, I grew up with my parents, brother and two sisters. Back then, Gravesend was what was known as a 'new town'. It was built specifically to house the overflow of the poorer areas of London. Morality was low and crime was high.

I was a very nasty little boy. My father used to beat me, and so I would take it out on my mum. She loved me, but I showed her no respect, I didn't want to know her at all. The aggression I developed became so intense that I once held an axe to her throat, nearly killing her.

Along with aggression came bad habits as I became more out of control. When I was just eight I had my first cigarette. It was my cousin Morris, who lived next door, who got me smoking, one day when we were fishing down at the canal.

It was whilst I was living on the estate that I began to hang around with a gang. We may have seemed like just a group of little kids, but our gang was vicious. We used to do dreadful things to people, and in our eyes they were just practical jokes. We'd go out and pour petrol through people's letter boxes, threaten to set people on fire, put nails under cars and attack other kids in the street. We even put rags in car petrol tanks and set light to them. If it were dangerous or caused people grief then we would do it, because we found it funny. I was a skinhead. Our gang looked very much like a lot of racist gangs, although it wasn't actually true of us. The truth was we didn't discriminate; we were against anyone who got in our way regardless of race.

By the time I was ten I had been expelled from every school I had ever set foot in. That makes it all the more strange that it is in schools that I spend a large proportion of my time today. Before I knew it, the local authority had decided that I should be put into a military-run boarding school. The school was located between a military hospital, a military prison and a place for people with severe disabilities. From the point of view of a ten-year-old, this place was like a freak hospital with people who had one hand five times the normal size, and an ear ten times the size it should be.

I was at Budleigh Manor School for Boys; it was like a prison camp! Being a boarding school, there wasn't much to do, and because it was situated in between all these other places, it made our lives even more cramped. This wasn't a good thing for us because we used to go glue-sniffing anyway. If there had been something to keep us occupied we probably wouldn't have done it, but there was nothing else to do. When I was in Gravesend, my mates used to talk about glue-sniffing, but none of us actually knew how to do it. It was at this school that I learnt how. I was proud that I broke the school record for absence in the time I was there. When I arrived, the record was something like three weeks, but I disappeared for about three years. I couldn't stand it there, so I ran away. When I got back to Gravesend, I taught my mates what I considered to be the only useful thing that I had learnt at school – how to sniff glue properly.

There were a few places where we'd go to do glue. We would go into the grounds of the infant school and the junior school, and sit in the bushes, sniffing. Having said this, I never really had any good experiences with glue. It was dodgy – we knew it could stick your throat together. We did it because there was nothing else, and because it got you street cred. I was the one who knew how it was done, which made me better than the others.

On one occasion, some of us had gone to the bushes in the junior school. We were doing glue, and the bag came round to me. But this time something happened. I remember falling over, and some glue came out of the bag and into my throat. I started to choke. The others just sat and laughed at me. I was really panicking, but they couldn't stop laughing. The glue was starting to set and so I'm coughing and spluttering and turning red, thinking that I'm going to die. Eventually I throw up a lump of glue, just like a cat coughing up a hair ball! How it came out like that I've no idea, but it didn't seem to put me off.

Another time we were there glue-sniffing, I was convinced that I had swallowed a spider. The glue was making me hallucinate. I was shouting, 'Get it out of me, I can feel it, it's alive! It's in my gut! It's in my gut!'

The girls were trying to calm me down, while my mate Monkey and a couple of the other lads were trying to hold me still. It wasn't difficult for them because my body was numb from the glue. I wanted to struggle but I couldn't move. Monkey looked down at me and smiled, 'It's alright mate', he said, 'I've just got to cut you open and get the spider out and everything will be fine.'

I was really frightened, and as he came closer to me with his knife the girls had to stop him. He thought he was helping me: the glue was affecting his mind too. It took a lot of talking to stop him from actually stabbing me. It was lucky really that the girls never did any glue-sniffing; otherwise we could have got ourselves into much more trouble than we did.

It probably sounds as if terrorising people and glue-sniffing were all that we did! But as part of the gang we used to go camping on the football fields and that sort of thing. It was trespassing, but it was doing things that normal kids did. We used to enjoy playing golf there. Somewhere along the line we had 'got hold of' a set of golf clubs, and we loved the game. We would go and play on the football field first thing in the morning before anyone else was around. There was a proper golf course alongside Lovers Lane, and there was a long barbed wire fence running around it. We used to go onto the course when nobody was around, through holes that had been made in the fence. We would go hunting in the brush for the old golf balls that people had lost, and then sell them to a bloke we knew in Gravesend. He would give us something like 10p for a Slazenger ball and 5p for a Dunlop ball, that sort of thing. It was in doing this that we realised that we could go there at four o'clock in the morning and there would be nobody on the grounds, which meant that we could play golf. We couldn't see the point in playing golf on a football field when there was a golf course standing empty. We had no respect for the place, teeing off from the greens and creating huge divots. We played there quite regularly during one summer.

One morning Monkey and I had been glue-sniffing, and we decided to go and play a bit of golf. As usual we went to use the hole in the fence to get onto the course. The trouble was that I was so high on glue that I missed the hole and walked straight into the fence, which was barbed wire. I was in real pain; my hands were cut to pieces. I was lying on the ground in agony, when suddenly I got it into my head that we had been jumped by another gang. I was hallucinating – it was obviously the glue screwing with my mind again. But when I came round, I just got up and walked off like nothing had happened. It came and went really quickly, but the thought that we had been jumped was so real at the time. I was still bleeding, but it didn't seem to matter, because we were there to play golf, and that was what we were going to do. My hands are scarred even now.

As we made our way over the golf course, we came across a ball stuck up in a tree. Obviously there was no way that whoever had hit it up there was going to go up after it. However, Monkey was like a gorilla – that's how he got his name – and he could climb up anything and everything. It would be nothing for him to shin up a tree and get a ball down, even when he was high on glue. However, this time something went wrong. As he jumped across from one branch to the next the branch broke and he fell all the way to the ground.

What made it worse was that he fell onto a stick that was pointing upwards. From where I was standing, it just looked like the stick was coming out of his side. He was crying out, making a terrible wailing noise. I was so high that I thought he was just having a laugh. It really did *look* like he was pretending, like when you're young and you pretend to be stabbed by holding the sword between your arm and your side. When I got closer I realised just how serious it was. The stick had gone right through his back, punctured his spleen and come out through the other side. My only option was to go and find the groundsman. It was really scary because we shouldn't have been on the golf course in the first place. The groundsman, however, soon realised the seriousness of the situation and my reprimand was postponed. The ambulance drove up over the course to pick up my friend. He was in hospital a long time and was left with a massive great scar all down his stomach.

Another place we used to hang around was at the paper mills. They were by the Overcliffs next to the hospital. The Overcliffs were massive chalk cliffs, like a gravel pit – but chalk. We made a den there out of the paper. It was quite a long trek to get there, but coming back, there was a short cut you could take. This short cut involved climbing up the side of the chalk cliff, shinning up a tree, swinging the tree from side to side, and jumping from the tree onto the cliff.

Then we climbed up through the branches then over B&Q's fence and home. Simple!

In those days, I was short and fat, but the others were all really skinny. Like I said, Monkey was like a gorilla, he could get up anything, and this one day at the paper mills, he had taken the cliffs short cut and had made it to the top safely. We took it in turns to get up there, like we always did. Everyone else was at the top by the time it was my turn. There was quite a crowd forming at the top, people who'd seen the tree swinging from side to side, wanted to know what was going on. My problem was that I was the wrong build for swinging on trees, together with the fact that I suffered from a fear of heights. So I approached the tree with a great feeling of fear. Awkwardly and slowly I made my way up the tree with shouts of encouragement from Monkey and the others above me. As I started swinging everything seemed to be going fine. Then it was time to let go. I jumped. Grabbing hold of the next tree there was a loud crack, it came away from the cliff and I started to fall. I landed on my head with a bang. Aware of the voices above me I heard someone saying that I must have broken my neck. I hadn't though; I just got up, dusted myself down and walked away with a bit of a headache. This was one of a number of times when I escaped death, when I should have been killed. I was 'lucky' – again. I didn't know it, but somebody was watching out for me.

There was one other place where we loved to hang out. It was in the big field behind the working men's club – the electricity substation. This substation generated the power for the entire King's Farm estate, which was thousands of houses. It was surrounded by wooden slat fencing (this was before they used barbed wire for that sort of thing). Outside the fence, you could hear the light buzz of the generators. Being a wooden fence, it was easy to get over, and on the inside, the buzz was really loud. There were four generators in this box with a two foot gap between each one, and 260,000 volts going between them. This was another of the places where Monkey and I used to go sniffing. He decided that by putting our heads between these generators on the inside, the buzz would go through us, making the 'buzz' from the glue even better. We started to do it all the time. One night, we were lying down in the box, looking up at the sky. It was a really clear night and the stars were out. It was an amazing sight, and we were loving it, soaking up the atmosphere.

Suddenly, I had an experience that really freaked me out. It looked like the sky was being ripped open. It was as if somebody had taken a knife and stabbed through the sky from the outside – the universe was open and I could see what lay beyond. Then some stairs started to descend through the tear, and there were eight golden lions on either side. As they came down, there was a glowing white figure who appeared at the top. The figure started to walk down the stairs towards us.

I jumped up. 'Monkey,' I said, 'did you see that?'

He didn't have a clue what I was on about. I was so scared that it was around this time that I stopped glue-sniffing totally. I realised how dangerous the hallucinogenic side of it could get, and how often I had come close to death.

Besides the glue, I had become obsessed with guns. I had a .22 air rifle, which was very powerful, especially for a young lad like me to be messing around with. It fired pellets, which were like real bullets; they could blow a hole in metal. We used to go hunting with it down at Cobham Woods. We would go out and shoot small birds, blowing them to pieces. We were so into it that we would go camping by the watering hole where the birds and squirrels went. I used to have some telescopic sights for the gun, and they were amazing, enabling me to hit a matchstick from metres away. These sights were spot on, which was bad news for the squirrels. My cousin Morris and I would go there and have a right laugh, with no concern for the wildlife whatsoever.

I became so competent with the gun that I could shoot hearts out of playing cards. And so one time, I got Morris to hold a playing card up in the air, while climbed up into a tree. I planned to shoot it from about forty metres away.

Bang!

'How is it?' I shouted to him.

'Yeah!' he replied, laughing. 'You hit it!'

And so I brought the sights down lower, until I targeted his thumbnail.

Bang!

I blew his thumbnail off, just because I could. I was horrible; I enjoyed my life, not caring about who or what I hurt.

Within my family, life didn't get any easier. When I was eleven I stabbed my brother, John, because he stole a crisp from my best friend. I had a lock knife which I threw at him and it landed in his leg. In response to this, my older sister stabbed me in the nose with a screwdriver.

My behaviour got steadily worse, until it got to the point where I threatened people non-stop; our neighbours, my mother, anyone. My mum had several nervous breakdowns, which were partly caused by my anti-social behaviour.

One day, I had decided I wanted to go out and buy some cigarettes or something, but I'd run out of money. I asked my mum for some money but she had said 'no'. I went totally

mad, shouting abuse at her and I went running
out of the back of the house. My dad was out
there chopping up some wood. He put out his
arm to stop me and I ran into it. For anyone
watching it would have looked like something
out of a cartoon. I swung all the way around his
arm and landed flat on my back. He was a big
bloke – he weighed well over twenty stone –
and he put his knee down on my chest.
Obviously he didn't put his full weight on me,
or I'd have been crushed, but he had me well
and truly pinned. I watched him pull his arm
back and I could see that he was going to punch
me. It was only my mum calling to him from
the house that stopped him from doing it. He
got up and I ran off down the garden. Even
then, I was shouting and swearing at him as I
ran. I jumped over the fence at the bottom of the
garden and gave him some lip. He came running after me, crashing through the fence, not
jumping over it. I just kept running.

I was only thirteen; but that was it. I was on
my own.

2

Doing the Drugs

The question now was 'where does a thirteen-year-old go when they've just left home?' I didn't have to go far, not even off the estate. I moved in with my girlfriend and her two young children. Her name was Sue and she was thirty-five. She had been going out with John, my brother, but I stole her from him; I looked after number one and didn't think of other people's feelings. It seemed fine to me that Sue would rather be with me than my brother, and he soon found himself another girlfriend called Liz.

Sue was a big girl; I liked large ladies, and it was when I was living with her that I got into a really heavy lifestyle. She got me into drugs on the one hand, and introduced me to mediums and the occult on the other. It all came about when she asked me if I'd done cannabis before, and I lied. So when she brought some gear home, I was put on the spot. I could hardly say 'no' now.

Sometimes, when you look back on your life, certain choices have been real crossroad decisions. And this was one of those stupid choices that changed the course of my life – everything went downhill from that one bad decision to smoke a joint, and be a real man.

And I really did want to be a grown-up. I wanted to work. I wanted to have my own family, but not being able to get a job, I had to do something to help support my new-found drugs habit and 'us'. This was when I started to steal big time.

There was a bloke who lived next door to Sue and me who was called Potter. He was bald and he wore John Lennon glasses. He absolutely stank of yeast from the home brew he made in his bathroom. Anyway, as well as a brewer, he fancied himself as a bit of a medium or clairvoyant. It was with Potter and Sue that I first did an Ouija board.

At first I was a bit scared, but it was quite funny to watch a glass shoot around on a little board. So Potter used to make a big thing of the Ouija board, and one night a message came up 'from the spirits' that the kids had fallen out of bed.

The kids were in next door, where Sue and I lived. Sue was quite concerned, and went to check on them. It turned out that they really had fallen out of bed, and so I started to think that doing an Ouija board was pretty cool. I thought that these spirits were really nice friendly people. I got really interested in the occultist arts and witchcraft in general. And in time, I was doing Ouija for myself and I really liked to know that the cards were on my side too. For the purposes of this book, my involvement in witchcraft doesn't need to be covered in graphic detail, but it did exist, and it played a large part in forming the person I was to become over the next few years.

It wasn't long before Sue and I split up. I moved in on Liz and quite soon, I moved in with her. For the second time I had stolen John's girlfriend from under his nose.

Liz was another large girl. She was twenty-nine and she had black curly hair. She always wore black. I loved the gothic look! She lived with her young son, just five doors away from my mum and dad's house in Raleigh Road.

I was still only a young teenager, but I was supporting a growing drugs habit. I progressed from minor stealing to doing houses over and doing other stuff with credit cards. I don't think I was very good at this point, because I got caught all the time! I used to get given fines, but I never paid them. Then they put me into care homes or Borstal. Nothing had any effect on me. Sometimes they would give me community service that would involve cutting grass in graveyards, pulling up weeds from between gravestones, helping out old people or mentally ill people.

There was one occasion where my community service was painting the inside of an old

church. The church was in a place called The
Valley, just off the estate. I was with a lad we
called 'Chopper'. He was a drug dealer, and a
good mate at the time. Neither of us really
wanted to paint, and when we got there,
Chopper thought it would be funny to slip an
acid into my drink without me knowing. It was
LSD, a 'blotter' called a 'superman'. I had no
idea that he'd done it, so I started to work,
painting the toilets in this church. We had a
supervisor with us, and he was walking around
the grounds with the vicar once we had started
to work.

I started to have some really weird feelings
that I couldn't explain. I started to be happy –
really happy. It wasn't like a normal kind of
happy; it was like a 'weird' happy. The colours
I was painting with were the lime greens and
pale yellows that you would expect to find in
toilets, really bland colours. I thought they
needed a bit of livening up, to bring a bit of
warmth to the place. Among the tins of paint
that we had been given were some brighter
colours, red, green and a sunshine yellow. They
were really loud and were intended for the
nursery for the children.

However, the state I was in, I thought that
they would make the perfect colours for the
toilets. I wouldn't normally have ideas like that,
but it just seemed like the right thing to do at
the time. Instead of *painting* onto the walls, I

thought that it would be great to simply open the tins and *throw* the paint over the walls. It totally went everywhere, not just up the walls, but over the ceiling and across the floor! It was running down the doors, dripping down the urinals and into the sinks. The room was covered in paint. I paused and stood back, looking around; I thought that I had done a masterpiece.

Behind me the door opened and I turned around. In stepped the vicar with my supervisor, looking around in complete disbelief. They stared at me, waiting for an explanation, and all I could manage to say was, 'What do you reckon? It really livens the place up, don't you think?'

This had all been Chopper's plan to get us both off community service by getting me out of my head, and he offered an explanation to the supervisor. He said, 'I think he's hallucinating.'

'Yes,' replied the supervisor. 'It certainly seems like he's doing something.'

Chopper calmed them down and told them he understood what was going on. He advised them that I should be taken home and they left it up to him to get me home safely.

So Chopper walked me as far as the end of the road and then dumped me. From The Valley to my house was roughly a twenty-five minute walk at the best of times. This was not the best of times.

I was fine until I got to the Kentucky Fried Chicken. Up until then the hallucinations weren't really that bad. It was when I tried to cross the road that my problems really started. I would just step off the pavement onto the road when I would see a car coming by. Every car that went by me would turn into some kind of stretched limousine in front of my eyes. I must have stood there trying to cross the road for the best part of an hour.

Then a kind old lady approached me, and she helped me cross the road. I turned to thank her, but when I did, her head turned into the head of a bear. The next thing I knew was that this old lady with a bear's head was roaring at me. I was completely freaked out by it and I ran away.

As I made my way home, I was looking at all the cars. One of them was an MG and it appeared to have a big grin across its face. Then all of the cars started to speak to me.

Considering that I had never taken anything like acid before, all this was new to me. It was the most bizarre roller-coaster ride. One minute I was terrified, the next I was enjoying the experience. It was all really weird. Everything seemed to be jumping out at me. Garden gates would be slamming and the pavement was rocking as I walked along it. It was like a big adventure, trying to get across the Grand Canyon or something. It was too much for me; I didn't have a clue what was going on.

When I got back to Liz's place, my head was really hurting. I couldn't control my thoughts so I went up to her son's bedroom. It had all the toys in there and I thought that it would be really calm and a great place to sort my head out.

However, I was on the bed, on my head, talking to the Peter Rabbit wallpaper, when little Ben came in, took one look at me and said, 'Daddy, why are you talking to the wallpaper?'

I had no idea what to say to him. I mean, kids talk to their toys all the time, but I was totally thrown by the question and I started to become very paranoid. I suddenly needed to get away from it all, so I convinced myself that I could fly. I got up onto the roof and got ready to jump off.

Everyone came out to look at me, which was quite embarrassing considering that it was the road I had grown up on. I knew all of the people and they all knew me. They were all shouting, 'Yeah! You can fly! Go on! Jump! You'll be all right! Go on! Jump!'

Liz knew all about the effects of acid, and she told me that if I jumped I would just end up a bloody mess on the pavement. It took her three quarters of an hour to calm me down, but I did come down in the end.

What made it worse was that day we had got her family coming over. So she sat me down in front of the snooker on the television. Ray Reardon was playing. He hit the ball and it jumped off the table, through our television screen and landed on the carpet in our living room. The referee came and knocked on the screen. It was strange; he politely asked me if I wouldn't mind passing him back the ball so that they could continue the game. There it was, interactive television twenty years too early! I didn't stop to think who might be around, so I went to pick it up for him. I got some really weird looks from her family. Liz's mum and dad really hated me that day, and I don't blame them.

Particularly after the way the glue had messed with my mind, you would have thought I'd have avoided LSD altogether. But, sadly not.

In comparison with glue, the trips on acid were powerful, so when I did get deeper into LSD, it was because the excitement outweighed the risk.

I remember going strawberry picking with my mate Stony this one time. We had been smoking cannabis, and we fancied having a laugh. I had been strawberry picking with my mum when I was little, and so we thought that it would be really cool to do it again. So off we went and had really great time. It was a nice day, we had a laugh and because of the cannabis, we felt like we didn't have a care in the world. I loved growing up in Kent – I can smell the strawberries even now!

When we finally decided to go home, I picked up my bike – Stony sat on my handlebars and off we went. As we were riding along we saw a big green bus, and I thought it would be really cool (as kids do) to have a race against it.

We were doing all right, bombing along the road trying to catch up with the bus. We overtook it, but as I pulled up in front of it, I hit the curb. I pushed Stony off the bike – I could see the driver wasn't going to stop in time.

The bus hit me, knocked me to the floor. The front wheels of the bus went over the bike, mangling the frame around my legs. The bus wheels, front and back, went over my body. This was a major accident on our estate – in fact, it would be a major accident anywhere. But again – somehow – I cheated death. 'Somebody' was definitely watching out for me.

The worst thing about the accident was that it happened at the end of Raleigh Road, and so when everyone came out of their houses to see what had happened, they were all the people I knew again, including my mum.

The thing that really sticks in my mind was that somebody was saying, 'Get some brandy! Get some brandy!' And I lay there thinking,

'Great – a free drink!' I was absolutely gutted when the brandy came out and was given to the bus driver – I was so hoping they were going to give it to me!

The ambulance came quickly, and the paramedics took the bike off me and wrapped me up in a blow-up plastic bag to protect my body from any further damage. They got me down to the hospital where I was examined and x-rayed. But amazingly there were no bones broken, no internal damage – nothing wrong with me at all, and I had to be discharged!

I never really had much joy with bikes back then; I was involved in a motorcycle accident on Drake Avenue not long after that happened. We nicked a motorbike from our estate. However, I wasn't used to that type of motorbike; it was big and you had to lean in to a corner to get it to turn. On a 50cc bike, you could practically steer it round corners; a manoeuvre which would be fatal on a more powerful bike. I was cruising along Drake Avenue, and I started to pick up speed. I was going so fast that I nearly hit 100mph. I was supposed to turn with the road, but I forgot to lean into the curve. But it was too late when I realised what I had to do, and I rode straight into a lamppost. The next thing I knew the ground was skidding along underneath my visor, literally one inch from my face. If I hadn't had a crash hat on, I would have left my face on the tarmac.

I thought that this time I must have done myself an injury, but when I checked – again there was nothing. I just went and got the bike from the lamppost and put it in an alleyway so the bill wouldn't find it. Then I walked home to Liz.

It was while I was with Liz that I got into credit card fraud. Everything was quite straightforward until we lost the card. We owed two heavies (who had just got out of prison) about £50. To cut a long story short, Liz and I split up and I moved in with a short slim Irish girl called Corrine. So when the heavies and their mates came looking for their money, Liz told them exactly where they could find me.

When they caught up with me I was given the worst beating of my life. One of them held my head tight in an armlock and another pounded me in the face with his fist and his knee. I must have fallen to the floor eventually, and one kicked my ribs in and another bloke broke my arm. In the background, I was dimly aware that Corrine must have called the police. And, strangely, they all stood by and waited for the police to turn up. The police came together with an ambulance. I was put onto a stretcher, only this time I really was dying. Corrine told the police that the men, who were stood around me looking on, were the perpetrators. But there

was no way I would have pressed charges;
these were very dangerous men and they really
would have killed me. Once again it was time
for me to run away, only this time I wasn't
alone. Corrine was coming with me.

3

Cars and the Quarry

Life was becoming too much for me to handle. The life of crime and drugs was putting a great strain on my relationship with Corrine. Even when we moved to Clacton in Essex to escape the heavies, there was a tension between us. I became so paranoid that it became unbearable for Corrine to live with me. We soon split up and I moved on again, to Maidstone.

It was while I was living in Maidstone that I had my first experience of needles. In comparison with the turn my life was about to take, the previous fourteen or so years of my life were an absolute fairytale.

One afternoon I had been out shoplifting with a friend. Roger earned his living by shoplifting whisky and other drink, and selling it for drugs. I went with Roger to his mate's house where there were five professional thieves – and me – sat around a table. I was easily the youngest, aged just fourteen. The others were aged between twenty and forty. The whole atmosphere was freaky.

The bloke whose house we were in was introduced to me as Shaggy. Shaggy was a drug dealer and he struck me as a recluse; he sat at the end of the table. His chair was like a throne; he looked quite distant and imposing. It was very clear who was in charge of this gathering.

I was shaking.

He slowly placed a box on the table. Opening it, he removed his works. I watched him prepare the stuff and stick the needle into his arm. I was totally out of my depth, and all at once I was filled with fear, but it was a sick fascination that made me watch, and for some reason, I couldn't take my eyes off him.

'All right', he said, 'who's for business?'

There was a glass of water on the table. I watched him flush the blood out of the needle. The water in the glass clouded with blood and I realised that we were all supposed to use the same needle. Shaggy passed the needle around the room. This was not a normal hypodermic needle. Shaggy was using a needle that dentists would normally use. It was the type that you have to use two fingers just to hold it, and your thumb to use the plunger. You could almost hear the sound as the needle broke the skin and went in. Shaggy, and I suppose others like him, used this needle out of choice, because you could unscrew the needle part from the plunger and just put another needle in. This was great for addicts, because getting hold of works was one of the hardest things.

Anyway, as he passed his needle round, he began to take orders for drugs. The next person took the spoon with the gear on it; he put in the needle, did his stuff, and after injecting he flushed it in the same glass as Shaggy had used. Two different types of blood were now mixed together in the water. The needle worked its way around the room, each person doing the same thing.

By the time the needle reached me, there were four different lots of blood in the glass. Even then (it was the mid-eighties), I knew all about AIDS. I was scared. I felt so pressured – I was with the 'big boys' now. The others convinced me that it was the right thing to do. Roger slowly wrapped the tourniquet round my arm, and I watched the vein jump up. He took the needle and pushed it into my arm.

Doing needles is like a severe version of drinking, stealing and lying, you know you shouldn't do it, but once you have, that's it; no turning back. And you can't change the past.

I often make the analogy that cannabis is like driving a Mini, whereas using a needle is like driving a Ferrari; however effective, the Mini will never be the same once you've driven a Ferrari. And so my life took another dive; and I began dealing drugs to support my growing addiction.

I moved in with a sixteen-year-old called Tina. It was while I was living in Maidstone with her that Liz got back in contact with me. She had been attempting to track me down to let me know that she was pregnant, and I had had absolutely no idea. In the course of time, Liz gave birth to a baby girl, Melissa, and during my time living in Maidstone, I used to go back and visit them occasionally.

I had also started to take advantage of people really badly. I had a friend called R.D., who lived with his girlfriend in the flat across the corridor from Tina and me. He was my best mate for a long time. We were the same age, we were both skinheads, and we did drugs together. One day he went out with his girlfriend and while he was gone I drank a bottle of his Southern Comfort. I knew that he would miss it, and so I had to do something to replace it. I panicked, and the only thing I could think of was to refill it by urinating into it.

When he came home, I was cutting the speed that I used to sell, and next to it, I had a big bag of glucose powder. He thought that the glucose powder was speed, so I sold it to him for £500. Then, with his girlfriend, he drank the Southern Comfort. I told them what I'd done, but they didn't believe me.

There was one time when R.D. and I went crazy. We had made a cocktail of glue, speed, cannabis and Southern Comfort, which got us totally out of our heads. We were out for a good time and it was like nothing could stand in our way. We went out in the evenings looking for cars – Ford Escorts Mark II, the easiest cars to steal. Then we would drive them to the quarry and smash them around. It wasn't a very big quarry; it was in the middle of a field, on a farm surrounded by woods. Rallying the cars round the woods was great fun, and then when we were bored with them we would tip them into the quarry and go out and steal some more. There were already five or so cars at the bottom of the quarry and then we just piled the others in on top. It was like a breaker's yard, there were fourteen cars in all.

After the day at the quarry I was feeling paranoid. I couldn't sleep and there was nothing I could do to calm down. I got out of bed and went to the kitchen. As I got myself a glass of water, my head was flowing with thoughts about the cars and how my fingerprints were all over them. I had to do something, but I didn't know what, so I rushed out of the flat and started banging furiously on R.D.'s door.

'All right, I'm on my way,' he shouted, but I just kept banging.

'Mate, open up, it's me,' I said, just as he was opening the door.

'Steve, have you any idea what time it is?' It was clear that I had woken him up and he wasn't happy about it, but that didn't matter to me.

'We've got to do something about those cars, our prints are all over them, and the police'll find them, and they'll be able to trace it back to us, and then we'll get nicked, and then...'

He looked like he was about to punch me, but he agreed with what I was saying, so obviously the drugs had started to make him feel paranoid too. We decided we had to act that night, so we planned to siphon petrol from the neighbours' cars and then go back to the quarry to blow away the 'evidence'.

When we got to the quarry, it was the early hours of the morning, but it was so dark we could hardly see what we were doing. We made a trail of petrol from the cars to the embankment where I thought we would be able to light the fire from a safe distance. Our intention was to light the match and then throw it down to light the trail. The problem was that it was very dark. There we were, throwing matches, but nothing was happening. R.D. made his way a little further down the embankment for a better aim, but as he did so he slipped, and I heard him roll down into the darkness.

The night was suddenly silent. I couldn't see him and I was confused. After a couple of minutes, I presumed he had got fed up and legged it home. I started to try to figure it out clearly in

my own mind. R.D. wasn't here, so it made
sense that he had gone home. Yes, that must
have been it, typical of R.D. to leave me to do
the dirty work; I would have to do the job
myself. This time I hit it lucky and threw the
match and caught the petrol. Not surprisingly,
there was a huge explosion. The cars went flying twenty feet up into the air; it was awesome.

To my amazement I suddenly saw R.D. make
his way up the embankment. He was back-
dropped by the inferno. When he had slid
down the bank, he had rolled under one of the
cars. He was in a terrible state, the back of his
hair was gone and his ears were burnt, his
clothes were smouldering. We sat and laughed
at the state of him! Maybe out of fear, or out of
relief, or out of adrenalin rush, I don't know
why we laughed, I can't explain.

However, the explosion must have woke the
farmer because the police arrived soon after
and tried to have me arrested on a charge of
attempted murder for what I had done to R.D.
When I realised how serious this was, I jumped
bail and ran away with Tina.

We moved down to Folkestone, near Dover,
to a place called Fort Road. We had got hold of
a Ford Cortina Mark II and drove all our stuff
down to a bed and breakfast – which was a bit
of a con because we never got any breakfast! I
was planning to start dealing down there; I'd
brought plenty of speed with me. I met someone

who was already dealing in cannabis, and so we set up a partnership. One day we broke into a car boot and got hold of two Purdeys – shotguns – with loads of cartridges. We took them to a quarry to have a laugh and practice shooting with them. We were trying to sell them on, but it turned out that they were impossible to get rid of; even then, they were both worth mega bucks. We had to break back into the car we had stolen them from, to put them back, because it would have been too dangerous for us to fence them.

We were ripping people off left, right and centre. We would go into bars and start chatting up the girls, claiming to be photographers for some big magazine. I'd tell the girls that my brother was the editor and then we'd go back to the flat and take loads of photographs of them when I knew Tina wasn't around. Life was just one big laugh at everyone else's expense.

I had this friend called Bunny, who was heavily into needles and that sort of thing. He seemed to be the only person that cared about the way I was living. He kept telling me that I was getting too far into it; the burglaries, and car thefts, the drugs – everything. He desperately wanted me to get away from it all, but I turned my back on his advice.

One day my 'business partner' and I had a big drug deal on, but it went bad. He had put everything he had into this deal, his flat, his television, and his stereo. When the deal went bad he lost out in a big way. We parted company swiftly and Tina and I moved back to Maidstone.

In Maidstone, Tina moved back in with her parents. Once again I was alone with nowhere to go. There was nowhere for me to stay in Maidstone, and with the police still after me for the incident at the quarry I had no reason to stick around. Not knowing where to turn I went back to my roots. I went to stay in Gravesend. I was going home.

4

Banged Up

My sister had become pregnant at fifteen and I remember hearing that the council wasn't obliged to give her a place to live because of her age. Because of this, my mum and dad moved out of their house – making themselves homeless – so that she would have somewhere to bring up her child. It was clear that I wouldn't be able to stay with her for long, and so I did something that I thought I was never going to do again.

Telephone in hand, I must have thought about dialling the number for the best part of an hour. Even when I did decide to dial, it took me three attempts before I actually got as far as completing the number. I still had my doubts when I heard the ringing.

'Hello?'

'Hello mum,' I said.

I had not tried to contact her for years, but I was desperate, I told her that I needed somewhere to live. They had found a job caretaking some bedsits, and as part of that job, they got their own flat in the block to live in. She told me that the landlord had another block of flats over the road, and that he was looking for someone to act as a caretaker there. It was cool and very soon I had a flat too.

Once I was in I went around the other flats introducing myself to the tenants as the bloke who would be collecting the rent. I knocked on one door and a girl with long dark curls answered. She looked like a hippy, all bangles and sandals and a long tie-dyed skirt.

'Hi, my name's Steve,' I said, explaining why I was there.

'Hi, I'm Heidi', she replied, 'thanks for calling round.'

She was trying to close the door, but I had already smelt an all too familiar smell and seen a packet of kingskins (large fag papers) on her bed. I knew nothing about this girl, but I did know what king size fag papers were for.

'I hope you're not smoking dope in there.'

'No, no, no,' she replied, looking very paranoid. I thought that I could hear voices in the room.

'Well, if you are', I said, 'I'd like you to invite me in so we can smoke together!'

And so began our shared cannabis habit, which moved on to speed and other stuff as our relationship in drugs developed. We began snorting, and when she wasn't around I continued to inject myself. I didn't realise that she was already into that as well because at that time, I knew nothing about her. It turned out that she had been in and out of clinics for years, and she'd had her first stroke in her early twenties. When I turned up on her doorstep, she had only recently come out of a clinic, so she was completely clean of hard drugs. Here I was, re-introducing the drugs into her system, even using needles.

Getting close because of the drugs, we spent more and more time together – to the point where we got into a sexual relationship. Heidi and I had a very open relationship. Basically we looked after each other sexually – no strings attached. It was a comfortable arrangement for both of us, we could do exactly what we wanted and neither of us would feel tied down. The thing was, we didn't need the open relationship, we were good together and we wanted to be together.

Heidi had no idea that I had jumped bail and was on the run, so it came as a surprise for her when I was arrested for something small and it was found that they had a warrant for my arrest for attempted murder! I had spent seven or eight months on the run and this counted heavily against me, together with the fact that the police had a statement from R.D. that I had intentionally tried to burn him. Not surprisingly, R.D. got a lenient six-months community service and I was put in prison, on remand.

The first thing that happens when you go into prison is they sort out your criminal record, and then you meet the people who are going to be your 'trustees'. The 'trustees' are prisoners who have served the majority of their sentence and are given positions of responsibility within the prison. It's all about giving people jobs in prison; most trustees are in on life sentences and have nowhere else to go. Anyway, their job is to get you through your first few weeks inside. This meant that instead of dealing with the prison officers (screws), you were dealing with other inmates. It is at this stage that you get given an official code.

You were given a certain code to protect your identity and to hide the crime you had committed. Only the trustees were supposed to know the code, but they would often tell the other prisoners, which wasn't good if you had been nicked for paedophilia or rape. These people were beaten badly. I, however, was on remand for attempted murder – which gained me a little respect. Nobody knew the circumstances, and so nobody knew that it was an accident. As far as anyone else was concerned, I had tried to kill R.D.

I was in a 9 ft. by 12 ft. cell, with three bunk beds, a table and a bucket (toilet). There were dirty pictures all over the walls. I walked into the cell and put my stuff on the table. I had my little radio, my soap and my toothpaste.

Looking around I thought to myself, 'Yeah, this is pretty cool. I can handle this.' I looked up and there was a bloke stood in the doorway staring at me. His face was completely tattooed up; all I could see was his eyes. My first thoughts were that he was either going to beat me, kill me, or take me for 'his wife'. I decided to stand up to him and be brave; the idea being that I might get a bit of respect for trying to defend myself.

He came in.

'I'm taxing your stuff,' he said.

I stared at him, wondering what he'd done to get put in prison. I tried hard not to let him see my fear.

'Over my dead body', was the thought in my head, but it also came out of my mouth. He came up to me, put his arm around me and, to my relief, told me I could share his cell.

It was a twenty-three-hour lock up, so we were only allowed out for one hour for exercise. For the first two weeks, I don't remember sleeping hardly. Tattoo-man was on the top bunk and I was on the bottom. All I was thinking was, any minute he would do me in. Then one day he sat me down and told me what he was in for. He had stuck a crowbar into a security guard's throat – he was never getting out of prison. After this heart to heart, we got on really well together!

I started dealing drugs in the prison, and Tattoo-man (one of the prison trustees) got me a job very quickly. I became a cleaner, which meant I went all over the prison, and I was able to pass around letters and bits and pieces like that, including drugs.

Tattoo-man and I shared a cell with a sixteen-year-old lad called Mutley who was in for shoplifting. I woke up one morning to the sound of choking. I turned on my light, which triggered a warning light outside our cell to alert the screws. I turned over and Mutley was hanging from the bars. His tongue was about six inches out of his mouth – it was horrifying. I went to help him but Tattoo-man grabbed hold of me. He was saying, 'If the kid wants to die, then let him die.' I couldn't move – he made me watch Mutley hang himself. The screws came in and got him to hospital. Fortunately, we heard was he was going to live. Even so, it was a pretty heavy image to have in my head, especially at such a young age.

From then on I picked up a load of new tricks in prison life. I was taught more advanced ways of how to break into cars and safes, and how to get around burglar alarms, that sort of stuff. I was still doing drugs like cannabis and DFs and eggs, but I didn't get involved during this time with needles, because they went round about forty people. It was far too risky, and I wasn't completely stupid!

All the young kids that came in on detention were given a hard time. I saw people being hit with snooker balls, all sorts. The really young ones were being raped in the showers and they had to put razor blades in their underwear in order to protect themselves. I heard of three or four suicide attempts; it was pretty awful. If I hadn't been in a cell with Tattoo-man then what was happening to the others would have probably happened to me.

I was called back to court three or four times. By this time, R.D. had told them exactly what had happened at the quarry, and he wasn't having any of the attempted murder stuff. Because of this, the charge was dropped to arson and I was sentenced to six months in a young person's detention centre in Gosport. Although I had been remanded in normal prison, I was too young to be sentenced there.

It was run by ex-military personnel and I was put on the experimental 'Short Sharp Shock' programme. The building was an old hospital. Our dormitory had a 10 by 80-metre parquet floor. There were thirty of us in each dorm and every day we had to polish our floor with a six-inch-square cloth. We did this three or four times a day, all the time we were there. It was hard work, and I hated every minute of it.

As well as this we had to do our work duties. We made sheets (for prisons etc) on a massive loom. It was all very physical. For what work we did we got paid in small plastic chips, and then on Friday you could spend your chips on shampoo and soap, or Mars bars and chews. But I really couldn't stand doing this work, none of us could; we were prepared to do anything to get out of it.

One day, I gave one of the blokes there my plastic chips to try to break my leg or my ankle, anything to get me away from that loom. I was literally paying him to come up behind me and cripple me. He made loads of attempts to break my leg and it didn't half hurt, but unfortunately it didn't break my bones. This meant that I had to carry on working, and my leg was killing me – but it had to be actually broken to get me out of the work. I'm reminded now of Peter Sellers and the hilarious Pink Panther films!

There were people taking more desperate measures to stop working. One of the young lads from my dorm convinced the screws successfully that he had appendicitis! They took him away to have his appendix out and he got to spend a bit of time in hospital, relaxing. We all used to fake illness to get out of work. That way we could sit in the hospital dorm messing around with the Ouija board.

I was really finding life in the detention centre hard going. When I had four months left to do I received a 'Dear John' letter from Heidi. She had been visiting me in the prison and in the detention centre, but she decided that she had had enough. She wasn't going to wait for me. It hit me really hard; I was devastated and I tried to hang myself. I got so bad that I was almost put into a straitjacket. They gave me counselling, which was really helpful, and after just two weeks of talking me through the problem, they had convinced me that my life was worth living after all. Those last three months saw a complete change in me. Because of my good behavior, I even ended up being number one cook, which was pretty cool. And the best thing was I'd given up smoking, and I hadn't been able to do any drugs while I was there. Basically, I had gone through all the withdrawal symptoms during the first few weeks, so by the time I was nearly leaving, I was sorted. I was seriously thinking about going straight when I got out.

I am totally convinced that the 'Short Sharp Shock' system worked. It was so short, so sharp and so shocking that I never wanted to go back there again.

There was a remission system in use by the government, for prisoners, which would get the sentence reduced by half. This was apparently to put an end to the overcrowding in prisons. If I got in trouble again after being released, I would have been straight back to finish my time. But there was no way they were getting me back in there!

They let me out a few days earlier than I was expecting. The day I was due to leave, they took me to the gate and gave me my grants and my old clothing. (When you have a programme of non-stop exercise eighteen hours a day, a lot of people in detention lose loads of weight. Because of this, they need smaller clothes when they are released, and that was the idea of the grants.)

Except, that is, when you're put under gate arrest – the one thing every prisoner fears! And I was no exception. On the day I was due to leave, they took me into a little room and they told me I was under gate arrest, and that the Essex police were waiting outside for me. The screws put a packet of cigarettes on the table in front of me and I was soon smoking them. The police took me to Clacton and I was put in a cell overnight. In court, the next morning, they had me on a charge for something I had done years before, from when I was with Corrine. It was something to do with a car I had had, a Triumph Herald. I hadn't had any tax on it, so I had taken the tax disc from another car and put it onto mine.

In fact, the case was so petty it was thrown out of court for being too old. But the gate arrest had thrown me so much that I quickly returned to my old thinking – and more tragically – to my old habits.

Having been let out early, there was some good to come from it. I was able to get back to Heidi before she left for good. She was going away to sort her head out, but I was able to talk to her first and I managed to convince her that it was worth giving it another go. So, with everything sorted out we thought we'd have a party to celebrate. I had a stash of drugs from before I was locked up, being looked after by a friend. I called Waz, another addict, so I could go out and pick it up.

Heidi and I were just on our way back from picking up the gear, with Waz and one of Heidi's friends also in the car. Waz was driving but something didn't smell right, and I didn't know what.

The Square was a main road and normally it was as busy as any other main road, but there we were with just one or two other stationary cars around us. I noticed Waz pull a wire from the ignition of his car ... I could smell the police before I saw them.

Heidi had a handful of cannabis, already cut up. Basically, if you're nicked with cannabis already cut, the police can charge you with 'intent to supply', instead of when it's uncut, 'possession'. With this much, Heidi could have been up on a charge of 'intended dealing'.

Then, several things happened all at once. Heidi's friend, the other bloke, became paranoid and ran away. As soon as I saw the police, I put half the stuff into my sock. I took the other half of the block and slipped it into Waz's pocket thinking, 'if I'm going down, then you're going down with me.'

Waz got out of the car and flipped the boot, which must have been a signal arranged with the bill, because they were all over us in two seconds flat.

Heidi got out of the car and legged it down the road. The police chased after her. She threw the cannabis she had into some bushes and kept running.

I got out of the car and the police had me slammed up against the side of the car before I could do anything. The next thing I knew, we were being rushed to the police station; Waz, Heidi, me and the other bloke. They split us up straight away. The other bloke was released immediately because he had no drugs on him, and although he was a dope-head, he really had only come along for the ride this time.

Waz had set us up, and the police were obviously expecting a really good bust. They told each of us that one of the others had told them everything and that we should talk as well. I knew that Heidi would never grass on me. They had talked to her; strip-searched her and found nothing. They only found an eighth on the pavement, which wasn't enough to do her. They didn't find the discarded lump in the bush and because of this they were ready to release her.

By this time, I hadn't even been out of prison 24 hours, so I was looking at going back inside for a long time. I had a block of speed in my sock worth about £2000 (or the equivalent of eight to ten years in prison). It became obvious the bill had a warrant to search my gaff, when one officer came into my cell and asked me, 'Do you want to be strip-searched here or in your flat?'

Knowing that I was carrying a potential ten years in my sock, I thought it was best to do it back at my flat, thinking I might be able to stash the gear somewhere on the way there. Well, the one thing that is supposed to be impossible to do is stash anything in a police car. Once you get dropped off, they're meant to search the car, so that people sliding stuff down the back of the seats get nicked for it. I knew this, and I was just sat in the back of this car, with the police, who were telling me what they expected to find at my place. I thought that I might as well get friendly with them. I had nothing to lose, so I started to fabricate what they'd find, and they got really excited at the size of the bust. They couldn't turn around to look at me, but they still wanted to hear what I had to say. They could only look in the mirror, so I asked for permission to lean forward. They were so excited, they said 'yes', so I leant forward. I kept talking and at the same time I slipped the block of stuff under the mat beneath the driver's seat.

By the time we arrived at my place, they were convinced they would find stuff everywhere, and that it would be a case of 'you name it, we've seized it'! To their complete disappointment, all they actually found was a few bits and pieces sat on the mirror. Waz had told them that I had loads of gear, but what he hadn't told them, was that I had been carrying it in my sock.

Anyway, as we had arranged, they gave me a strip-search – the full Monty – with rubber gloves and all! It was all very humiliating. Of course it was all for nothing. They told me to put my clothes back on, get back into the car and they were going to take me back to the station. They were so annoyed at having found nothing, they were thinking more about Waz, and whether he had stitched them or not. I seemed to have been forgotten! This gave me the chance to reclaim the block of speed from under the mat in the car. I slipped it back into my sock.

Half an hour later, I was back in the cell. A different officer came in and started having a right go at me.

'You said we'd find the stuff on him!'

I remained silent.

'We didn't find anything!'

I listened with great interest.

'We even took him to his flat to search him and we didn't find a thing!'

'Who do you think I am?' I said finally.

I must have looked quite pleased with myself. This bloke clearly thought I was Waz. It was brilliant, a huge mistake on their part, which confirmed to me what I already knew – I had been set up.

Before long I was put into a cell with Heidi. We got talking about what had been going on and it turned out that when they searched Waz, they had found the stash that I had planted in his pocket. The police didn't take too kindly to this, and saw it as him trying to get one over on them by setting me up. He got six years in prison for it.

Normally, in the 'underworld', you wouldn't let your mate go down instead of you. You'd cover for each other. But in certain circumstances, like this one (where I was stitched up for a reward), it was OK. And the others thought so too, especially as Waz was the type of person who thought it was fair to shoot   people with a crossbow, if they owed him money or dope.

Anyway, we were taken to see the Chief Inspector. There I was, stood in the Chief Inspector's office being given a caution – and unknown to him, having a lump of speed in my sock. It shows the sort of nerve I had, how devious I could be. We walked free, and to top it all off, later we went back to The Square and found most of the stuff that Heidi had thrown away.

This was one of the most character-building periods of my life. Sadly it failed to create a very pleasant character. Instead of learning a valuable lesson in prison, I had learnt different ways of bringing out my darker side. Free from prison at last, for the first time in a long time I could sit back and enjoy life. There was nothing to run away from.

5

Spells and Speed

The depths I was sinking to were at an all-time low. With Heidi, my life became 100 per cent drugs and crime. It wasn't helped by the death of Melissa. She had choked on a toy in her cot. I was so young to be a father, but when she died, I was devastated. I didn't have a job – I didn't need one, because the stealing and the drug dealing brought in all the money I needed.

At this time, I also had a little black Mini. Obviously I still wasn't old enough to drive it, and I had stolen it from somewhere, but that didn't make any difference to me. Not once did I ever have any trouble from the police – or anyone – about the car. In fact, I can remember on one occasion, when I was living in the Mini, on a very cold night, the police knocked on the window, to see if I was alright. I appreciated it.

I absolutely loved the car! It had a scaffold pipe for an exhaust – but I was never pulled for it. And it was mega loud! One time, I bought a couple of cans of black spray to smoke out the windows! Only I hadn't realised you needed special spray to do it. I had the only car in Kent with 'Jet Black' windows!

It was good to have the car because it made stealing easier. There was one time, where some mates and I had gone to the Isle of Sheppey. I'd heard about a bloke there who sold acid, and so we'd gone to score some 'blotters'. We drove down in the Mini and got the stuff off him. He told us we would be hallucinating in around twenty to forty minutes after taking one. So we 'dropped' the tabs before we left, thinking that by the time we got home, the effects would just be kicking in.

On the drive home, I remember UB40 were playing on the radio. I was a big fan of UB40 at the time. At the top of town, Pier Road, there was a double crossroads and some traffic lights. The lights were red, so I stopped the car. Then the 'fun' started, as the traffic lights began to flash to the beat of the music. It was really confusing; I didn't know whether to go, stop or what to do. My friends were no help; they were totally tripped out in the back of the car. I had never seen anything like it before in my life, and all of a sudden an arm appeared to be coming out of the side of the traffic light and it waved me on as if it wanted me to go. I put my foot on the accelerator, but there was something inside me that told me that this wasn't right, and so I stopped. It was a good job I did, as there was a Tesco delivery lorry coming along the road and it would have easily hit us. I have the feeling that we would probably have been killed if I had kept going. At the time I believed I was in control. But the truth was, my life was well out of control, and I was a danger to myself and to others.

However, in a very short time, I went on to other types of acid like 'microdots' and 'window panes', which were far more dangerous again, and I was in a self-destructive spiral.

One day, Heidi and I dropped an acid and went out for a walk. I started to get hungry and so we went to a café by the clock tower for something to eat and I ordered a cheese sandwich. It was one of my favourite things to eat. I remember biting into it, and I could feel something start to move around in my mouth. It was horrible; I spat it out onto the table to have a look. This wasn't the right thing to do, obviously, because the place was really busy and there were kids near us, running around. The people I was with knew I was tripping. I could see the sandwich moving on my plate and I was so out of my head that I began to try to complain to the manager. I was convinced they had sold me a maggot sandwich. Of course they hadn't, and so we got thrown out for being weird.

It was one of those times when you really didn't need to bump into anyone you knew! And while we were walking down through the town, we bumped into Heidi's mum. It was quite funny; Heidi was forever saying that she always saw her mum when she'd just done an acid. You really don't need to bump into your parents when you're tripping out of your head. Heidi's mum was a lovely lady, and when we met her in the car park she expressed a desire to buy Heidi some new clothes. By way of a fashion note for the younger readers, in the early 1980s fluorescent colours were very popular and everything you bought was really brightly coloured.

Well, I walked into a shop with them and everything was fluorescent; the skirts, the shirts, everything. Because I had dropped an acid, I felt like I was spinning around in the middle of the shop. The colours were flying everywhere into a giant blur, and I felt like I was going mad. The people watching assumed I was having a panic attack, and Heidi's mum was quite worried about me. In reality, I was trying to dodge the T-shirts and skirts that were flying at me from every angle! Heidi told her that I wasn't feeling very well. It was all very embarrassing.

In this period of my life, Heidi and I had also collected a library of books on witchcraft and the occult. Not that I could read brilliantly, but I had all of the books. Heidi was well into it as well, and we would sit down together and do stuff like try to spin coins with the power of

your mind. There were loads of spells and spirits you could ask to help you to become a better
person. I thought that it was great.

I have seen various things happen on the
Ouija board through the years. There have been
record players starting and stopping, things
crawling across the ceiling, things banging on
the ceiling, doors and windows opening and
slamming shut; it was very frightening and
nasty.

Mixing the occult with drugs was even more
dangerous. It seemed there was a strong link
between the two.

One night Heidi had been working late and I
had been using the Ouija before I went to bed.
That night was strange – for some reason, the
Ouija board didn't 'behave' itself well, and it
freaked me out, to start with. It was very scary
when I went to bed, and was pinned down in
my duvet by a heavy 'presence' and I could not
move at all. I was aware of the fact that there
were hands around my throat, and I could not
breathe. In my head, I kept repeating, 'O God –
help me. O God – help me.'

The 'presence' lifted and looking back again,
I am aware of the fact that 'someone' was
watching over me, and this time, I made the
connection between the prayer I had said in my
head, and the help I got.

This encounter with the 'other side' had
scared me so much that it was the furthest I

ever got into the occult. After that I steered clear
of the Ouija, and stuck to what I had found to
be less threatening.

Meanwhile my needle situation had become
so bad that I could inject as many as ten times a
day. I had no other choice but to inject, because
I was no longer able to snort any drugs. I had
completely wrecked my sinuses and nasal
membranes, which is very common. There are
three major veins in the human nose, and every
one of them had been destroyed because of
snorting. At this point, I tried heroin, but it
made me feel very sick. We injected speed and
coke, and we would crush up downers and
inject them; I even tried injecting alcohol. Even
when I didn't have any drugs I just wanted to
flush something through my blood. I would
flush glucose through my system, stuff like
that.

But there was still a side of me that was
acting as a conscience. Despite everything, there
was an element of my personality, which saw
that although what I was doing was destroying
myself, there was no reason for me to go out and
ruin the lives of complete strangers and I was
very safety conscious when it came to certain
things. I always remembered a news item on the
television about a dustman who picked up a bin
bag, swung it over his shoulder and was
stabbed by a diabetic's needle. This image was
very vivid in my head. I never wanted to be

responsible for something like that. So when I had used my needles for the last time, I would bend the end around and stick the cap back on the end. This meant that even if the cap came off, the needle wouldn't hurt anyone. Of course, once these needles have been bent out of shape, they're obviously not easy or safe to re-use.

I used to get our needles from the bins at the back of the dentist's, (this was before the introduction of the hygienic yellow boxes) and we would re-use what he had discarded.

Heidi and I were living in a place where seven or eight people would come around on a regular basis for sessions. We smoked joints all day every day. We had the works; bongs and shotguns, pipes that cannabis is smoked through, and we would use it all. In the centre of the room we had a washing up bowl – our ashtray. It was full of half eaten sweets and rubbish. We would empty it into the dustbin, but the bowl wouldn't get emptied for days at a time. In the kitchen, we had half-eaten cans of beans which had their own little botanical gardens growing in them; mugs were infested with mould and other nasties. Once a needle was used for the last time, it was thrown into the rubbish bin. There were times when I would run out of needles, and so there was only one place to go to find them – the dustbin.

Digging deep in the rubbish, fag ash and dog ends to get to the needles, I would find them

covered in bean juice and all sorts of grotesque
creations, which festered in the rubbish. Once I
found one, the needle would be taken to the
tap, washed off with water and then straight-
ened out with pliers ready for use. It was complete madness that I even tried to do this and
Heidi certainly never knew about it. These needles were designed to be used only once, possi-
bly twice at a stretch. After that the end bends
over like a miniature fishing hook. Injecting like
this is like pushing a ballpoint pen into your
vein. It hurts. Then you would rip the vein trying to pull the needle out again. This is what
would cause bruising and even some veins to
collapse.

The worst scenario was to have the needle
snap off in your arm. If that happened then you
were in real trouble, because the needle could
actually go into the bloodstream and follow the
flow of blood until it could go no further.

I got to the point where there were scabs all
over my body. I had no track marks because I
wasn't a heroin addict, but the damage I did is
still visible today. My veins are dark and lumpy.
They should be smooth, but mine are swollen
and horrible. It is what is known as a collapsed
vein, and I have got them all over.

When the needle breaks in and out of the
vein, the vein repairs itself, getting thicker and
thicker. It becomes so big that it collapses. This
makes it harder and harder to inject and so I

had to pick the scabs sometimes, to get the needles in.

I shared needles all the time, and so I was very fortunate that I never contracted the HIV virus, especially when the needles were only flushed through with tap water between users.

'Someone,' without doubt, had his hand on my life.

6

Fantasies

By 1986 Heidi and I had had enough. We realised that our lives had reached a dead end and we needed to get away from Gravesend and the drugs scene. Heidi was holding down a job as the manager of a superstore in London, and so we moved up to Lewisham so that she could be nearer her work. Times were changing. I found myself another job as a caretaker, which meant that, again, accommodation came with the job. The flats were over the top of a parade of shops and a car showroom. Things were at last looking up.

The plan for a drug-free life was not to last long. We discovered that there was a dealer living just around the corner from the flat. Instead of a nice fresh start, we tended to save loads and loads of money – and then just go and spend it all on drugs. Part of the plan for our new life involved my getting a proper job.

One morning I looked out of the window of our flat at the construction site over the road. A group of people were buying old buildings and refitting them, turning them into flats and selling them on. I went over to them and asked if they had any jobs going. They asked me what I could do and I bluffed my way into working for them. I told them that I could do anything. Nowadays I can actually do all these jobs because I have done them, but at the time I was 'jack-of-all-trades and master of none'.

At first they had me working as a general labourer. They gave me a little blue Ford Fiesta van, insuring it and taxing it for me. This helped me do all the running around for them, picking up all the bits and pieces that they needed for each job. Then, when they moved on to the next job, I would get left behind to do all of the finishing off, like painting or plumbing or whatever. This was all great, but when I started on the drugs again I became very paranoid. I thought that they were going to sack me and take back the van.

For a time, Heidi and I had been intending to save up some money and go off backpacking around India, doing the bit that hippies do. We managed to save around two grand. One day I came home from work and I told her to get her bags packed. I was so mixed up and paranoid that I told her we should leave while we still had the van. Strangely, she agreed and the next thing we knew, we were off to the airport. We had no tickets and no destination, but we did have the van! It was so exciting; the adrenaline was really pumping and we had £2,000 in our possession!

When we got to the airport we parked the 'stolen' van in the car park, got on a plane and headed off to Amsterdam. Our original plan was to go on to India from Amsterdam.

Amsterdam was a real experience. It was all sex dens and strip shows; there were prostitutes on every corner where we were staying. There were cafés that sold pot off a menu – it was a paradise for a dope-head like me. We managed to score rock cocaine and later almost got stabbed by the same gang who sold us the coke. I think they were after our money. It was very scary, but still very exciting and I learned a lot. The place just sucked us in, and drained us of all our money. When the money ran out, we realised that we were not going to make it to India this time; we would have to come home and face the music.

Before we left, I decided that it would be nice to take a souvenir home, so I bought some African bush seeds. I was smashed out of my head; Heidi and I had just done the last of our dope at the airport, and I managed to convince myself that they were just seeds, not anything serious. Heidi knew I had the seeds, but she didn't know that I was also carrying Indian opium in my camera – enough for just a couple more joints.

We got on the plane and flew back to England.

On arrival, we picked up our bags and went through customs. We headed straight down the 'Nothing to Declare' route without giving it a second thought. Everything was going really well. That was until I heard the voice.

'Excuse me, sir!'

Instantly, I started to sweat. My pants stuck to me (if you know what I mean!). 'Surely, there was no way he was talking to me.' So I ignored him and just kept walking.

'Could you come back here please sir?' said the customs officer, louder. This time I turned to look and I could not pretend that he wasn't talking to me. My thoughts were all over the place. I though that this was it. Getting done for drug smuggling would put me away for good this time. So I pulled myself together and turned back to where he was standing.

'Is this yours?' he asked, showing me a passport, 'somebody had found it earlier and handed it in to us. We thought we may be able to catch you here.' I had a short lecture on how I should be more careful, but it was nothing compared with doing time for smuggling. I was free to carry on!

It was such a relief. I couldn't believe how jammy I had been. Heidi was just as amazed. The trouble was that it really hyped us up again and we both got really excited. As soon as we got back to the van, we were expecting to get busted for TDA, assuming that the police would have been looking out for it, and us. Of course, nothing happened. But it was still really exciting; it was like being on the run all over again! We were half expecting something to happen to us when we got back to the flat, but again nothing happened. Two days went by and then the blokes from work came over to pick up the van. It had never been reported as stolen, and they were absolutely cool about it. I had had such a paranoia trip – over nothing.

I didn't grow the African bush seeds in Lewisham, but I did take a slight change in career. I found myself a little job with a dry cleaning firm in the West End. I was working with the rich and famous in London! All right, so I was only the driver; I delivered and picked up clothes to be cleaned, that sort of stuff, but it was great. I got to brush shoulders – very briefly – with loads of big names: Jonathan Ross, Cilla Black, David Jason, Michael Ball and Dustin Hoffman to name a few. Their costumes had to be cleaned specially, and that was my job. I used to go into their dressing rooms, sit down with some of them and we'd have a chat and a cup of coffee. Then I'd be able to get some posters and autographs, all that kind of stuff.

It was while I had this job that Heidi and I developed something of a taste for the musicals up West. For some of the shows we got to see, there were people on year-long waiting lists. I guess it was one of the perks of the job. I remember particularly going to see the *Phantom of the Opera*. When the performance finished I was the first on my feet – clapping, cheering and whistling, probably the only one cheering and whistling – but it was brilliant!

Eventually, I was sacked from the dry cleaner job for smashing their van up, on a little 'excursion' with Heidi. So I went on to work at a big firm in Bishop's Gate in Liverpool Street, London. I started out as a lagger, putting insulation on metal skirting before they built on it. The good thing to me was that I was also doing a lot of business with drugs, as a sideline. I was getting a lot of money from it. I was earning a good legitimate wage, and the money from the drugs was like a bonus.

I was supplying all the lads at Bishop's Gate with speed. This meant they did double the amount of work, because they had more energy and 'buzz'. There was one welder – the gaffer, actually – who was well into speed. He asked me to go and work for him. The job involved no work; all I had to do was supply speed on his building site. He was well happy – he had a gang of lads with a productivity that made him look great. He paid me a full welding wage and he let me keep all the profit from the speed. I was raking it in. The downside for me was that as a result of the contact with the drugs, I was getting heavily into it again myself.

I was still on acid doing 'windowpanes'. They were strongly hallucinogenic. One time, I had been watching Aliens, and then I dropped a windowpane watching *The Never-Ending Story*. I was so out of it, the dragon in the film flew out of the television and started to fly around the room. I was well excited by this. I knew it wasn't real, but the drugs take over your mind and you get lost in it. Normally, you know what's real and what's not, but the two start merging so that you cannot tell them apart anymore, and then you end up living out the fantasy.

After about an hour and a half, it all went scary. The dragon's skin began to flake away, and then he split in half revealing the alien underneath. It was horrible and I ran off and hid. The thing was, everywhere I went to hide, it managed to find me. It would come out of walls, come up out of the toilet, and this went on for about twelve hours. What had started off as fun became a nightmare that I will never forget – I couldn't escape from it and it wouldn't go away.

I used to live my life on LSD back then, taking anything up to four or five acids a weekend. Trips would vary wildly. I could be sat in a room, take an acid and any other people in the room would disappear completely. Obviously, they would still be there, but I wouldn't be able to see them. I could be tripping for close to twelve hours sometimes, and all the time, there could be other people there and I wouldn't know. So to have people disappear was just fine for me, and if somebody disappeared I'd just assume they had gone home. There were times that friends would say, 'I'm just going to the toilet,' and I wouldn't see them again. I would be thinking that it was a little bit strange, them going to the toilet and then going home without saying goodbye, but that was the drugs. They controlled your mind, you were so out of your head.

There were times that I would say to Heidi, 'I'm going down to the shops, I won't be long,' and I would disappear for a couple of days. In Lewisham we were practically living on top of the shops. But I'd close the front door and stand there, just outside, thinking: what am I doing? Where am I going? What was I up to? Am I coming in or going out? Have I already been to where I was going, or am I coming back?

There was one acid tab that took days to take effect; I thought I'd been sold a dud. I spent the evening watching horror movies and, like most people when their minds are full of scenes from horror movies, I went to bed following a certain routine. I stood in the doorway to my room and I judged the distance from the light switch to the bed. With the light on I would go in and pull back the covers on my bed, then I would go back to the light switch. Turning the light off

I would jump across into the bed, pulling the covers over me as I did so. Simple enough, and when I do my lectures in schools today, everyone seems to relate to this quite easily. But this one time I became conscious of the covers moving. It was like somebody was trying to pull them off me. I had a look over the top and, to my surprise, I found myself face to face with a three-foot scorpion. It was pretty awesome.

Like I said, the trips would vary wildly. I had one trip where mushrooms started to grow out of the carpet in my room. Then they opened up and hundreds of little glass butterflies flew out of them. I was transfixed by them, it was such a wonderful sight. Some trips weren't so good. I've had blood dripping through the ceiling, people peeling their skin, and there was once a room filled entirely with spiders. That was really freaky, these spiders covered the carpet, they were up the walls, there were even spiders walking around on the ceiling and falling off in clumps. It was terrifying; they climbed up my trouser legs, completely covering my clothes. I could feel them walking across my skin. I tried to scream, but when I did they ran into my mouth. And if that wasn't bad enough, there was no escape; the windows and doors had vanished. I ended up trapped in the 'spider room' for hours.

On another occasion Heidi got some acid from a girl at work. When we were living in

Lewisham we used to have people over all the time. We lived in the top flat. Although we had a doorbell, people used to throw stones at the window to get our attention because I used to disconnect the bell when I didn't want to be disturbed. This one time, I was sat down preparing a load of joints. (I knew we were going to be doing some serious acid that night and that it would be totally impossible to skin up later on, so I did it all in advance to save a lot of mucking about later.) We were sat talking, we'd taken the acid and we were waiting for it to take effect.

Someone threw a stone at the window. This is not a good thing; when you're doing acid you don't want interruptions, so we ignored it. Usually the person would just go away. At the time the stone hit the window the person shouted, and so instinctively we both looked across. I was certain I could see the blue flashing lights of a police car. Being the paranoid person that I was, I thought I heard a bloke shout, 'Come out, it's the police!'

I crept up to the window and looked out from behind the curtain. All I thought I could see was a police car with its light flashing. Every car up and down the road was a police car, and all the cars in the car showroom below us were police cars. And a bloke outside shouting, 'This is the police, come out with your hands in the air!'

I told Heidi that it was the police and we wasted the next six hours cowered in the corner waiting for the police to come up and bust us. I can't remember which of us finally had the guts to get up and go and have a look. For those six hours, we were more than hallucinating, we had also become acutely paranoid. The next morning the same bloke came over. He owned a shop down the road. He told us that he'd come over the previous night to score some gear, and that he wanted to know why we hadn't let him in. It was quite funny, he said, 'I knew you were there, I could see you looking out of the window at me.'

Not long after all this, Heidi got pregnant. This came as quite a surprise to both of us considering that Heidi hadn't had a period in ten years because the drugs had screwed up her entire body. It was incredible really, and we had no idea how it happened (so to speak!). Anyway, when she found herself pregnant she decided to stop doing drugs. I thought that that was cool. In 1989 Heidi gave birth to Marie. After this my perspective changed slightly.

For the two or three years we were living in Lewisham I had been scoring, selling and doing drugs. Now we had a dealer on the corner of our street. I became really annoyed by this. Not that he was interfering with my business, but I thought that it was well out of order that I was expected to bring up my daughter in an environment where dealers hung around on street corners! Once again I felt that it was time to get away.

We went for a holiday that summer, to Dartmouth in Devon where Heidi's mother lived. I loved it there. We stayed in a little fishing village where nothing ever seemed to happen. There were loads of boats and fishing trips. It was great; I told Heidi that this was the sort of place that I wanted to live in. She wasn't so keen but I talked her into it, and we ended up moving down, not to Dartmouth, but to Torquay nearby. She went down first with Marie to get settled, but I had to stay in London for two or three weeks to tie up the loose ends.

So there I was, in London alone, with just a credit card to keep me company. In our last few months in London, Heidi had been able to get hold of some personal credit cards; something that I was not able to do because of my form. And of course, she didn't have a criminal record; she was a manager of a big superstore.

Giving me the credit card was probably not the most sensible thing that she had ever done. I had an idea that it would be really original to buy loads and loads of stuff on the card, and then report it stolen; that way I figured I wouldn't have to pay anything back. So I bought about a couple of grands' worth of stuff. By the time I left London my debts were running into the thousands, and I had a lot to run away from. The trouble was, I started to become very sloppy in the things that I was doing. For example, I stole one of the cars from the car showroom underneath where we were living. I did put it back again afterwards, thinking that nobody would notice, even though there were an extra 400 miles on the clock. I was starting to get caught. I had spent my last few nights in London on the floor of a mate's flat. I had ripped everyone off, and some of these people were heavy duty, and they were after me. I had to get away from my own flat because people were turning up with pickaxe handles with nails sticking out of them, they wanted to do me in real bad.

Two or three days before leaving London, I stole a racing bike. I thought that I might need some transport. I used the bike to get to Victoria Station. I put it on the train and finally I was off to Torquay. It was a relief. I thought to myself then that when I hit Torquay I would never take another drug or commit another crime.

To reach Torquay was brilliant: the English Riviera. My new home was a five-minute walk from Torquay railway station. I had to go down along the sea front and pass by some arcades. I wasn't entirely sure where I was supposed to be going, so I stopped off in the arcade to ask for directions. I hadn't been in Torquay for more than an hour when I met my first drug dealer.

When push came to shove, I just couldn't break the habit, and against my better judgement, I scored some gear and I took it with me up to the flat. Heidi and I did some dope just to celebrate our arrival in Devon.

It's hard to imagine, but from that moment on, things got worse. There I was in Torquay, kidding myself that I had finally managed to break away from the drugs and crime that had had such a hold over my life for so long, but between 1991 and 1993, life went downhill all the way.

7

Breaking In

It was December 1992, just before Christmas; Heidi was having a bad back problem and was rushed into hospital. I was supposed to be looking after Marie, but my lifestyle wasn't compatible with looking after a three year old child, so she went to stay with her Nan in Dartmouth. I was at home alone.

It was at this time that I had recently met a group of girls who were heavily into raves. There were five of them; they were all very different, but each one was attractive in their own way. One day, they came round to the flat wanting cannabis. I didn't have any at home, but I went to get some and delivered it to them. They asked me if I wanted to go to a rave with them. I had never been to a rave before and I thought it sounded like a bit of a laugh. I mean – the idea of going out with five good-looking girls was great. They told me that they would show me the ropes and look after me; and so the following Thursday we went out.

They took me to The Blanford Inn which was a trendy bar, with really loud rave music and a small dance floor. It's not there anymore, it got burnt down a few years later, but it was cool. I sat in a dark corner at the back of the pub, with one of the girls. She gave me my first ecstasy tablet, smiled and kissed me on the cheek. She whispered in my ear that I would enjoy it, and that she would look after me once it kicked in. There was a load of loud music going on and the girls left me on the sideline and went into the rave to start dancing. There were at least seventy or eighty people jumping around in this little place. I took the tablet and I was sitting there waiting for something to happen; I really didn't know what to expect.

Before I knew it, my feet were tapping, as if I were listening to an Elvis song or some Country and Western music. I couldn't help it. Then the next thing I knew, I stood up and moved around like some kind of robot. I could not keep myself still – it was as if the beat took over my whole body. It was really weird. People were coming up and asking me if it was my first time; I think it was obvious! Within a couple of hours – that was it – I was a raver. I was totally in to it.

The sensation was strange, but it did feel like pure ecstasy, at the time. The company was great, I don't mean the five girls, and I ended up ignoring them for most of the night.

I was off talking to everyone, and we were all shouting and dancing around. I can recall the music being turned off, and that my body just kept on dancing. The girls told me that this night had just been a warm-up and that we would be off to another rave the next night. For four or five days in succession, we raved every night.

The first time, I had taken just one ecstasy, and then I had another half later on. Very quickly, at the end of that one, I'd take another, and then the next day I'd take another two. I was having to take more and more. It was like an addiction.

I borrowed someone's car because we were going to a rave in Weston-Super-Mare. There were hundreds of cars and people, queues of cars trying to get in. Apparently, the police were stopping vehicles, but we were already inside, so we were fine. I was sitting in the chill-out room, and I honestly thought I was in heaven; the combination of everything that night was like the best drug I'd ever taken. I was still smoking cannabis, but it wasn't really having any effect because of the ecstasy. It was a feeling that I struggle to put into words.

'Someone' was most definitely watching out for me on our journey home. I was so out of my head that the drive back was a nightmare. I was driving and I did manage to get us back to Torquay safely, but how I don't know.

The girls told me that that was how they lived. They planned their raves like holidays and booked time off work just to recover. They explained that that was how they worked it, going out raving every now and again in bursts, so many times in one week and then nothing for a while.

But I was stuck at home for the next couple of days and I found myself drifting into a depression, starting to become very angry inside. I couldn't work out how I felt, any of it. The comedown was too hard.

By the time Heidi got out of hospital I had become very aggressive and extra paranoid. I wanted to know what was happening to me, so I tried to find out what the ecstasy tablet was made of. I located the girls and they sent me on to their dealer. I knew him already, and he told me what the tablets were. It turned out that they were 90 per cent heroin. I had accidentally become addicted to heroin through doing ecstasy, and when I stopped taking the tablets, I started to suffer heroin withdrawal symptoms, which are horrible.

Around the same time I had managed to find my way into an organized fencing ring, where I would steal things down in Torquay and they would be shipped up to London to be sold on. Heidi knew nothing about this (she didn't know a lot of stuff I was up to). I started to 'take over' car parks, stealing from cars. We had control of the car park in Abigail Road. We would 'sort out' anyone else who we caught trying to steal on our patch. It was people like me who created the need for the police to install surveillance systems and the CCTV. I became obsessive; robbing and cheating, there came a time when I was breaking into places just for the hell of it. I learnt most of my job from my time in prison. I was told the best burglaries to do were the ones where you could go in, steal something and then come out again without anyone ever knowing that you were there. Several times I broke into places and I was stealing stuff with the owners asleep in the same room. I was also dangerous. The drugs made me feel that I was unstoppable, and I believed I could get away with all of it. I was fortunate that I did get away with it most of the time, but things didn't always turn out the way I thought.

A friend and I had planned a robbery from an insurance firm (the friend is now dead – drugs). We had an insider who told us that on a certain day there would be X amount of money in the safe. All we had to do was get in, empty the safe and get out again. Well easy! And before we did the job we had a bit of a smoke, just to calm the nerves. However looking back, it was probably a bit too much of a smoke. We reached the back window of the building and all we had to worry about was getting into the basement. Our information told us that there was an alarm, but that on this one occasion, it would have been 'forgotten' to have been switched on. There was nothing to worry about – taking the window out was easy, and it wasn't long before I was in the basement, torch in hand.

I was more than a little surprised, however, to find myself face to face with a domestic washing machine and tumble dryer. Looking back, there was nothing to make me think that it was an insurance firm at all. At the time, though, it didn't click in my head, and I took no notice. All we had to do was get upstairs and empty their safe. I started to walk up the stairs with my mate coming up behind me acting as a lookout. We got up to the landing, and then in to the main room. I was taken aback by the decor. This place was done out like a living room! I was thinking what a cool office it was, assuming that it was like a waiting room with magazines on the table, comfy chairs and a television. Then the truth dawned on me. It was the wrong place and we were in the house next door!

By this time the bloke who owned the house had appeared behind me, and my mate had legged it. I didn't know what to do; I stood there transfixed like a rabbit staring into the headlights of an oncoming car. He was shouting 'What do you want?' when I suddenly snapped out of it. I obviously had to get out, and quick. I just ran in the same direction as my mate. The thing was, the stairs to the basement were really low, and I was going so fast, that when I ran down the stairs I hit my head on the ceiling and knocked myself out. I fell the rest of the way down.

The next thing I knew my mates were waking me up, and I was not in the basement anymore. They'd come back for me and had dragged me out through the window and across the road, into some alley. My head was spinning, but it was a good job they did come to get me, because we saw the police car pull up outside the house. We were close to being caught this time. I had started to get careless in my work, and we were making mistakes.

A few times we carefully broke into homes using all our skill and discretion, only to find that the house was already empty. My job got quite frustrating, but it had become an obsession. I remember the last job I ever did, when I was really out of control. This story is one of the occasions where I – even now – become sad at the depths to which I went, because of the grip of the drugs.

I broke into a bungalow. I entered into the main bedroom and there was a crippled woman laid up in bed. The ironic thing is that I didn't steal anything from her, I just trashed the place while she screamed. The adrenalin was like a massive power surge, and when I broke into a house, I would feel as if I was in control of the place where people were at their most vulnerable. By stealing nothing, I was letting people know that I could get into houses if I wanted to.

For the victim, the fear comes from the knowledge that someone has violated their home. It was evil, the way I could shatter the confidence of people that I never knew.

The reader should understand that I am so sorry I have done these bad things. My behaviour makes me ashamed now and I don't tell you these things lightly – in fact, some stories have got the better of me, and I have taken them out of the manuscript, because I can't bear the thought of what I was doing then. But so that you understand the power of the addiction to drugs, I am telling you the stories. All of them are true, although I have hidden all of the names that would give away locations and peoples' identities. Through the years, I have seen otherwise normal people completely change their character because an addiction has taken control of their lives.

8

Out of Control

I used to sit down and think to myself, what will I be doing when I'm forty? I wished that I could stop doing what I was doing, but then I just took more drugs and forgot about it. I was trapped in my way of life, and I was driving Heidi up the wall with it. We would have big arguments. One time she turned round and hit me with a broom handle. She gave me a locked jaw and I had to go straight into hospital. The doctors had to peel my flesh with my ear away from the bone, dislocate the jaw and pull the cartilage out, then put the ear and skin back down on the bone and staple the join together. It was absolute agony, and has left a scar down the side of my face. So they sent me home with 40 ten-milligram morphine tablets to ease the pain.

Well, one day I was so depressed, that I downed the whole lot.

As part of the lecturing that I do today, I talk in front of a wide variety of people. I've spoken at business lunches and schools and all kinds of places. There was one occasion when I talked in front of a group of doctors. When I told the story of how I took the whole prescription of morphine, one of them said that 40 of those tablets were strong enough to knock out a herd of elephants.

Anyway, as soon as I had downed the tablets I went out for a walk. From St Luke's, the hill where we lived, to the sea front, there were 192 steps. It was called Rock Walk, and was next to the arcades, and the place was lit up at night with green, red and blue lights. I had made it all the way down, and gone all the way along the gardens and over the big footbridge to the beach. By the time I got to the beach, my body was totally relaxed, and my legs were shaking. I started to give out. I hit the ground with a bang and I remember it really hurt, especially my face. Then nothing.

When I opened my eyes I found myself back outside the flat with my key in the door. I've got no idea how I got there, and when Heidi opened the door to me I had this look on my face as if to say, what am I doing here?

I must have looked a right state, because she said I looked like I needed a sleep. So I went to bed. (The last thing you're supposed to do after taking an overdose is to go to bed; you're supposed to do everything you can to stay awake.) But, when I woke up a few hours later, I had a bit of a headache, but otherwise I was fine.

I had taken enough morphine to kill myself, but all I had was a headache. 'Somebody' had stepped up their protection over me!

Heidi was getting to the end of her fuse. She was becoming desperate to prove to me what a monster I was.

We had been into the occult together, and I used to invite spirits into my body. These spirits were supposed to help me to become a better person, and for this reason I badly wanted to be possessed. I thought it was the answer to my problems, but in fact it actually caused me over time to become more and more aggressive.

I met a medium who was meant to be the best in Torquay. I went to see her a few times and she told me that I had a spirit guide called Robert. This spirit guide apparently used to be a photographer. I never understood why she told me that he was a photographer. I thought that it was quite bizarre, but I felt no reason at the time to doubt her. I started to watch films about different types of witchcraft. There was black witchcraft and white witchcraft; it was said that there was a difference between the two – but there wasn't really. I was absolutely convinced that I was a 'white witch'.

I started to spend more and more time in my bedroom meditating, humming and speaking to all of those weird things, which I believed would help me become a nicer man. I must have done this over a hundred times. I was trying to make myself better financially, sexually, morally, everything.

The last time I went to see the medium, I was feeling very depressed. She read my tarot cards for me and evidently I had a rosy future lined up. She told me that I was going to do a lot of travelling and that my life would be great. Robert was looking after me and so I wasn't to worry about anything – the standard lines! She told me that I had everything to live for, but she didn't seem to have the power to offer me the hope that I was obviously searching for.

I had lied to Heidi saying that I was working as an 'odd job man', when in reality I was doing the burglaries and fencing stolen goods. I didn't really think it would make much difference how the money came in, just as long as we got it.

She wasn't stupid and could tell something was up with me. I couldn't help stealing from everyone, and she caught me out by marking some of her money. She left her purse on the table and, of course, I stole some dosh. I thought that I was being really clever because I had only taken part of the money, not knowing that she had marked it. She confronted me, saying exactly how she had caught me out. I was gutted; it hurt so much to know that she'd been able to do this to me, and I turned nasty.

Back then I weighed about seven and a half stone, not unusual for someone on speed. (I'm

6 ft. 3 in.) Heidi was roughly eight stone and about 5 foot six inches. I was so annoyed with her trickery, I saw red. I picked her up above my head and I threw her down the stairs. Then I turned on Marie, and I almost punched her. I almost punched my own daughter. And I would have done, if it hadn't been for Heidi yelling from the bottom of the stairs, '*Who are you?*'

It was the strangest thing and I'd never been able to work it out. I was thinking, 'What does she mean, "Who am I?"' And then I started to think really seriously about it. Who am I?

The only way I can explain it is to say that up until that moment, something had always had control over my life. At the age of eight, I watched a film about a man who had sold his soul to the devil. I was so impressed with it that the first thing I did afterwards was go upstairs in my bedroom and make a deal with the devil myself. But at that moment, when Heidi asked me who I was, I felt as if my mind had been given back to me, and for the first time in years, I felt alone in my head and able to make a 'good' decision. It was only for a short time, but it was long enough to stop me from punching Marie.

There I was, standing at the top of the stairs thinking, 'Who am I? What am I doing here?' It felt for a moment that whatever had been controlling me had let go. There was blood, and

Heidi was crying. I just kept saying, 'What am I doing? What have I done?'

Our relationship was falling apart; I could see that. I needed her help to get my head sorted out. I told her that I could change, that things would be different. Of course, she'd heard it all before.

But this time I was serious. I really couldn't handle who I was, and I don't blame her for rejecting me. Eventually it came to the point where I had to sit down and work my life out. There I was, on my bed, going over it all in my mind. I thought about my family, the stealing, the drugs, prison, Heidi and Marie, everything. After everything that I had been through, all the things I had done, all I could hear in my head was a voice, and it was clearly telling me to kill myself. I was thinking, 'Yes, that's exactly what I need to do. I need to kill myself. If I do it then I'll have nothing to answer for.'

It was then that I realised just how badly I needed to get my head sorted out, and my life. The only thing I could do was to find some space for myself. So I moved out of the flat.

9

Plans For the End

While we were living in Torquay, Heidi had been working in a hotel. I got on very well with the manager and his wife. I got on especially well with his wife, Teresa. They had tried to help me sort myself out. Teresa wasn't aware of the whole drugs situation, but she did know we were having relationship problems, and rather than getting a flat when I moved out, she told me I could stay in the hotel rent-free. I had got another little job as a handyman. She thought that if I made no alternative plans, there might be a way for Heidi and me to work things out fairly quickly.

It wasn't long after making these plans that Heidi and I finally split up. I was aware of the fact that I had to build a life for myself now. I applied to go to the local college on courses for plumbing and bricklaying. I knew that I couldn't use my head, but I could use my hands. And I did really well, getting into the routine of going in every day; I honestly believed that I had got my act together and that my head was sorted out.

And then the cheque arrived. I received a grant for two terms at the college all in one amount, and I couldn't help myself. I blew it all on cocaine in just one short week. It was as if the other person had taken control again, just as I had sorted everything out. I became frustrated again, and I started to have an affair with Teresa; everything began to fall apart all around me once again.

This time when I sat down to sort my head out, it wasn't to rebuild my life, it was to kill myself. I was looking for the perfect suicide.

Having been a drug user for so long, I knew exactly how to do it. I'd tried it before with the pills, but this time I didn't want to survive. I didn't want to have to explain to everyone why I'd attempted suicide.

I had been watching some American true murder cases on the television. I had become obsessed with them. I used to love the idea of people going out to kill other people. In a way I found it a turn on – it excited me; it got my mind going and got me thinking.

I vividly remember one case about a man who had ripped off the Mafia. He planned to kill himself in a hotel, but he accidentally left his key in the door on the inside so that they knew he was there. The chambermaid found him and called for an ambulance. They brought him back to life and he ended up going to prison and the Mafia killed him on the inside. If he'd placed the 'Do Not Disturb' sign on the door, he would have been able to decide his own fate. I knew that when I did it, I didn't want to go making any stupid mistakes, so I knew I had to plan it carefully.

For approximately two months I lived in the hotel with the knowledge that I was going to kill myself. During this time I tried as hard as I could to lead a good life, trying to be really nice to everyone, so that nobody would suspect a thing.

On the day I had chosen, I left the hotel with a joint of cannabis. The joint was for the night porter. I gave one to him most nights, and I explained to him that I would be heading into town to the clubs to do a bit of karaoke. He saw me leave.

I crept around the building and let myself in the back way. Because mine was the basement room, nobody knew I was back. I locked my door from the inside and I carefully took the key out of the lock.

I had a sink at the end of my bed with a little table underneath it. On it was an ounce and a half of amphetamine sulphate and ten hypodermics. I filled each of the needles up with the speed.

It was all very calm and calculated. One by one I shot myself up with the needles. I must have used about eight of the ten, and with each one I injected I could feel myself going more and more. After a while I fell flat on the floor.

Meanwhile, Teresa apparently had a gut feeling that there was something wrong with me. She had rung the night porter to find out how I was. He told her that the last time he'd seen me, I'd been fine, and that I had gone out for a night on the town. Even so, she wasn't convinced, and told him to go down to the basement and check my room. Reluctantly, he came down and knocked on my door but there was no response. He went back upstairs to let her know.

This is where the story becomes more difficult to relate. From here on in, I think it's enough to say that the truth is often stranger than fiction – and these details are given truthfully.

The next thing I knew, I was standing in the corner of the room. I could see my unconscious body, lying on the floor with a needle sticking out of my arm. Incredibly, I was separate from my body. When the children in the schools ask me what it was like, the example I use is that like in the film *Ghost*, when the title character gets shot, his body drops to the floor, dead, but his spirit keeps on running and he doesn't realise that he is dead. So there I was, looking at my body on the floor, and I was conscious of the fact that I could see myself dying.

Teresa still wasn't happy. She knew that there was something seriously wrong, and felt that I

was in the hotel, so she sent the porter down
again. This time he looked through the keyhole.

This was where I had made my mistake. My
body had fallen inconveniently right into the
middle of the room, and he could see me. He
took out his master key and unlocked the door,
but he couldn't open it because it was bolted
from the inside. He went away to call the emer-
gency services and the manager came down.

I saw everything that happened after this. It
was very surreal but also very real. I watched
the door to my room slamming open and I
watched the ambulance men come running in. I
saw them pulling the needle out of my arm and
checking my pulse. It was bizarre seeing this all
happening to me, right in front of me. I even
saw the manager come in, lift up my body, give
me a slap across the face and call out, 'You can't
die here; it would be bad for business!'

I was still looking on as the paramedics told
him to leave me alone, and I saw their efforts to
try to resuscitate me. It was really scary because
I was conscious of the fact that I was just spirit.
When I heard them say that there was no pulse
I remember thinking 'Wow!' and I started to
wait for my spirit guide – Robert the photographer – just like I'd been assured he would be
there for me. I believed wholeheartedly in rein-
carnation and the idea was that my spirit guide
would come and take me on to my new life or
plane or whatever! There I was waiting, but

nothing happened and no-one arrived. The weirdest thoughts started to hit me, I was thinking, 'If I am going to be dead now, and I am not going anywhere, then when they bury me I am going to be stuck on top of my grave forever.' What made this all the more strange was that I was looking at my lifeless body while I was having these thoughts. With no spirit guide, no sign of anyone at all, my beliefs had gone right out of the window. I was scared, more scared than I had ever been – and I think I had a right to be.

The paramedics strapped my body into a stretcher chair to get me out of the hotel. As they moved off, my spirit followed my body. When they took my body into the hallway, my spirit (the real me) suddenly became aware that there was something behind me, drawing me. I didn't hear a voice or anything, I just felt drawn. This is very hard to explain in words. I turned to see what it was.

It was a door. A big white door with four panels and a golden handle, suspended in mid-air with an incredible bright light creeping out from around it. In spirit, I went towards the door and I put my hand out to touch it. Before I could, the door melted away. Little did I know at the time that what lay beyond the door would change my life forever...

10

Light and Darkness

Looking in behind where the door had been I could see thousands and thousands of people. There was a golden path, which seemed to go on for miles and it led to an enormous golden arch. There was an incredible golden light which was really amazing. The faces on all of the people were unbelievable because they were all so human, yet at the same time they were unlike any human faces I had ever seen. They were not blemished in any way; they were as pure and perfect as a person could look.

Every one of them had their hands up in the air and they all had an expression on their face which made them look both happy and sad. They appeared happy, I thought, because they were there, but I felt that they were sad because I was not joining them. The image of the faces before me was so intense that I wanted desperately to be there with them, but I couldn't. I could feel everything; I was standing there looking at them. I wasn't exactly talking, but I was definitely communicating to the people that I wanted to be with them. A heart to heart kind of communication.

I looked down and I saw a big black hole immediately in front of where the door had been. Before I could do anything, I started to experience the overwhelming blackness and I was 'sucked' in, close to the hole.

We all have fears of some kind, whether it is enclosed spaces, spiders, drowning or other forms of death or whatever. There is an infinite number of terrors in our lives. My own personal fears were to lose my sight, to be deaf or to lose all sense of feeling. The worst thing that could ever have happened to me would be to have all three happen, and that was what it was like in this hole. It's difficult to explain, however. It was as if my mind was the only part of me that was still alive. I could not see anything. I could hear nothing. I could feel nothing. All I knew was that I was falling into the hole, and that I was very alone.

I also knew that I could well have been left in there forever. I don't know how I knew this, I just did. In truth, the blackness experience may have only lasted for three or four seconds, but it seemed like a lifetime. I had often joked about 'going to hell' – but in all honesty, I had never known anything as horrifying as the loneliness and blackness that surrounded me at that point. This was an experience I wouldn't wish on my worst enemy.

The next thing I knew I was in the ambulance watching the men working on my body, talking to me and then we arrived at the hospital.

11

Another Chance

My body was put onto a trolley and taken into the hospital. I was attached to a machine by wires and stuff. One of the nurses came up to my body and she poked me in the side. As she did this, the real me suddenly went back into my body. I can remember seeing myself, then feeling the nurse poking me, then I opened my eyes (from the inside) and she said, 'You're back then?' But all I wanted to do was sleep.

The next time I woke, I was still in the hospital, attached to the machine, and I could hear it beeping steadily. I opened my eyes and saw all the wires and patches stuck to my body. I could see the machine pumping up and down and I had a drip running into my arm.

I was scared. I still had the image of what I had seen behind the door in my head and I wanted answers to put my mind at ease. I freaked out, ripping all of the wires from my body, blood from the drip flicking everywhere, and the beep of the machine becoming one loud continuous noise. The nurses rushed in and they pulled the curtain around me. I was swearing at them and being very abusive. In fact, I gave the nursing staff a very hard time indeed. I'd like to say sorry to them, for what I put them through at that time. I desperately wanted answers to explain the things that I'd seen, and I was very confused, but they obviously didn't have the answers I needed. I felt the need to try to find someone who did. I went to my locker to put my clothes on – a pair of ripped jeans and a T-shirt – and all the time they were telling me that I was a sick man and that I was in no fit state to leave.

I struggled to put my clothes on, saying, 'I've got to get out of here!' But I could hardly walk. After all the things my body had been through, I was in no condition to go anywhere. My weight had gone down to about six and a half stone – quite a fragile weight! My body just did not function properly any more. My kidneys were on the point of giving up and I was regularly passing blood. I still had blood leaking as I moved, but, even so, I still managed to get all the way to the visitors' day room.

By the time I got there, two very enthusiastic-looking psychiatrists had intercepted me. It was quite clear to me that they were trainees. They were very efficient and very enthusiastic, firing loads of stupid professional questions at me.

'Did you see a tunnel?' one of them asked.

'No,' I said, 'I didn't see that.'

'Are you sure?' asked the other. 'It's very common. A lot of people do see a tunnel.'

'No,' I said, 'I didn't see a tunnel.'

'Did you see anyone you know?' asked the first.

'Any deceased friends or loved ones?' asked the second.

'No, no, no, I didn't see anything like that', I said. 'Why don't you let me tell you what I did see...'

'Did you see yourself being operated on?' one said before I could finish my sentence, 'because that's very common when you're dying; to see yourself being operated on.'

'Are you listening to me?' I snapped. 'I didn't see any of that. Let me tell you what I did see.'

And so they did. They sat and listened whilst I went over the thousands of faces behind the door and being sucked in the hole.

They thought my story was really weird. All they could do was suggest that I go down to the Specialist Unit on the outskirts of the hospital and see the head psychiatrist.

After a short walk down the corridor, I was there. I had an appointment to see him immediately. I sat outside his office briefly while the two trainees explained the 'situation' to him. When I got in to see him he had already supposed that I was mentally very ill. He really wanted me to tell him that I had seen a long tunnel with all of my loved ones waiting for me at the other end, but I couldn't, because I hadn't. I told him all about what I had seen happening in the ambulance, with the men working on me, and he agreed that there was no way that I could have guessed all that. He called for the ambulance men to come down and verify my story, which they did.

He then suggested that I should be admitted to a psychiatric ward as a voluntary patient. In fact, he told me that if I didn't sign myself in, they would have to section me under the relevant Act of Parliament. I told him that I would like to think about it, and so he let me sit outside his office for a minute.

While I was sat there I heard a little voice inside my head telling me to run. It wasn't like those old voices that I used to hear all the time; this was the voice of reason. I remember agreeing that it was the right thing to do, but I couldn't run, I could barely walk!

The head honcho's office was right next to the main entrance of the annexe, and in the other direction was the main part of the hospital. I tried to run up the corridor and I made it into a lift. As I got into the lift, half of my body went completely numb. I think I probably had a stroke. I was only twenty-six. I fell to the ground. I remember some people finding me shortly after, but they must have taken one look at me in my ripped jeans, stinking of pee, lying on the floor, and I don't blame them for walking away. Then one of the porters found me and lifted me up. He told me 'don't worry' and he muttered something about 'a stroke' and put me in a wheelchair and took me to what I think was the heart unit.

The staff there did some tests on me and they put a tablet under my tongue to get my metabolism going. While all this was going, on the psychiatric nurses were scouring the grounds for me. Of course, the last place they would have looked for me would have been the hospital itself. They were running around the grounds and I was in the heart place for a good couple of hours.

As soon as I felt my fingers and the rest of my body coming back again – which was a kind of miracle in itself because normally if you have a stroke there is at least some permanent damage done – I got up and walked out of the hospital and made my way over to the bus stop. Somehow, I caught the bus into the town and phoned Teresa.

She really helped me and managed to fix me up with a bed and breakfast in Belgrave Road. When I arrived at the B and B, I went straight to bed and I think I had the best sleep that I have ever had. I closed my eyes and I was gone! I was totally exhausted.

But yet again, I woke in the morning to the familiar voice in my head telling me to kill myself. It was the same voice that had told me to kill myself the previous time, and it just kept repeating itself over and over getting gradually louder and louder, 'Kill yourself! Kill yourself! *Kill yourself!*' It became so strong that I started to want it, and so this time I knew that I had to get it right.

First of all, I had to get out of the bed and breakfast because Teresa knew where I was, so I stood the chance of being found and rescued; something that I did not want to happen again. Fortunately, Belgrave Road is one of those places where there are quite a number of hotels and bedsits. I was lucky enough to find bedsit two or three doors down the road. The place was owned by an Irishman who didn't live there, and he only came by once a week, so I knew that there would be no way on earth that anyone would find me.

Well, I had already seen him that week, so I had six days of nobody knowing my whereabouts. I moved in straight away. Then I phoned Teresa from a phone box, just to let her know that I was all right. I really wanted to tell her where I was staying. She begged me to tell her and I desperately wanted to, but I couldn't get the words out. She started crying and I started crying – I was really panicking because I knew this time that it was really going to happen.

Then I went back to the bedsit with the needles and the drugs. The time was about midnight. I took out a photograph of Marie and

I thought about what her life would be like when she grew up.

I imagined her being asked questions about her dad, about what her dad did for a living. I saw her having to tell people that her dad was a robber and a drug addict, a liar and a cheat. Then I thought that if I were to kill myself, I would actually make life better for Marie and Heidi. That way if someone asked her what her dad did, she would be able to say that he had died when she was very young – end of story. It would save them both the grief of living with who I was.

So there I was, sat there ready with my needles, all set to get pumping away.

I don't know why, but oddly I started to think about the things I had seen last time I had overdosed, and suddenly I realised what it was I had seen. It had been heaven and hell. This stopped me in my tracks, because I was getting answers to the questions. The realisation of what I had seen made me stop what I was doing, and I couldn't bring myself to inject.

One thing was certain out of all of this – I was never very good at committing suicide.

12

The Choice

I had no way of knowing whether or not I had seen heaven or hell because I never knew anyone who had been to heaven and hell and lived to tell the story.

I had never thought about God in a real way before. I had always prayed when I was in prison – everyone prays when they are in trouble – but they were empty prayers. And I was always blaspheming and it meant nothing to me. This was the first time that I had thought that there could really be a heaven and hell, maybe that was what life and death were all about.

It was like my eyes and ears had suddenly been opened. The truth was falling into place, and for the first time in my entire life, all the confusion disappeared. The Bible says 'you shall know the truth and the truth shall make you free,' (John's gospel, chapter 8, verse 32) and suddenly I was free to make a decision.

At the same time, I felt like I was in the room with God and the devil arguing about me, and it was really weird.

I could hear a voice saying, 'Follow me and I'll give you love.'

And there was another voice saying, 'Sell your story – take the money.' When people die and come back to life it makes a pretty good story and I could have got a few hundred pounds from the tabloids. This voice did all it could to appeal to the greed for money that had constantly ruled my life.

But the voice offering me love was from the person who really knew what the root of the problem was.

The Bible says that there is 'spiritual warfare' going on constantly between the devil with his angels and God with his angels and that people are the victims of the devil's actions. And it was like it was going on in the room. Obviously I didn't see them, but there were two personalities present, who wanted me to belong to them.

On one side I was hearing 'love', and on the other I was hearing 'money'. It seemed like it was going on for ages: love, money, love, money, love, money.

It wasn't really a difficult decision to make. The voice offering love was superior. At about three o'clock in the morning I was moved to shout with all my strength, '*Love!*' It was no contest!

As soon as I did it, I was lifted up like a baby from a cradle, my feet were off the ground. By the time I touched the ground again, my whole and entire life had changed – completely.

Firstly, all the effects of the drugs, the physical cravings and even my mental addiction disappeared. I knew it was real when I found myself taking the drugs from the table and flushing them down the toilet. I had never, ever, in my entire life flushed drugs down a toilet. They were costly and I would never do that. But I wanted to get rid of them.

After that, I went back and picked up the needles. I ran outside and put them all down the drain. I don't know why, I just knew that I didn't want them near me again. It was just like everything that I was, became new. I felt like a new person. Everything I had ever been, fell away.

I was a new person. Where there had been hatred and insecurity, suddenly I was full of love. I clearly remember sitting in my bedsit looking at the wardrobe. How many people sit and look at wardrobes? This wasn't the nicest of bedsits by any means, but I was thinking, 'I really love that wardrobe!' I had never had that sort of thought before. Then I started to work my way around the room: I love the carpet, I love the television, I love this whole room, I love the cockroaches, I love living, I love this voice that says 'Follow me and I'll give you love', I love love. I love love.

I loved feeling this way. And I knew I was deeply in love with the person who had done this for me.

But I had never felt this kind of love before and I realised I wanted to share this love with someone who understood. I had this idea that maybe I should go and phone a vicar, but I was also starting to wonder if this entire thing was one big dream. I could almost have been convinced it was a dream because it seemed to be too good to be true! I decided that I would tell my name to every person I spoke to from this point onwards, so that when I contacted them again, I would know I hadn't dreamt it.

I went to find a church and I took down the number for the minister from the board on the outside. I went to a phone box. It was about ten past three on a Sunday morning which was far too early for him, and he didn't want to speak to me at that point. He told me to come to church in the morning. I was gutted. But instead I decided to move on to another church and get a phone number from their board. Exactly the same thing happened again. I didn't understand why a minister's job couldn't be 24 hours a day, seven days a week, and I felt I should not have been turned away.

But I'm glad that God had his hands on me – especially at that point – because I was starting to feel downhearted. But I just knew that God wasn't turning me away, and I still wanted to tell someone.

As I was leaving the phone box I caught a glimpse of an advert for the Samaritans. It said that they were there to listen and so I phoned them. I spoke to somebody called Richard, and I spent an hour telling him as much of my life story as I could. And then I told him what had happened earlier that night. He said, 'It sounds like God has got a call on your life.' I didn't understand, but I liked the sound of it. He told me that it sounded as if I had been 'born again' and was now a Christian (see John's gospel, chapter 3, verse 3).

I didn't know what a born-again Christian was; I had never heard of them. I'd seen my fair share of *Songs of Praise* when I was growing up, but I had never heard of that expression. My whole body shook with excitement and I was thinking, 'Yeah! Great! This is brilliant! But what's a born-again Christian?'

I may not have known all the words that Richard used, but being a Christian sounded really good. It turned out that he was a Christian too, because he had also asked to experience God's love.

Eventually he told me that he had to go. I wanted to meet him, but of course I couldn't, it is the Samaritan policy – and to this day I have never come across him.

When I put the phone down I was thinking, 'Yeah! I know God!' Even now, it's still a kick to know God.

I started walking back up Belgrave Road to the newsagent's. It was still early, and inside there was a man sorting out the Sunday papers. To look at me, I was in a right state; I had my ripped jeans on and I stank, but I still needed to talk about this love-experience, so I went up to him and started a conversation; 'Do you believe in God?'

'Yeah, I believe in God,' he said, but I must have totally freaked him out.

I sat my ripped jeans down on his freezer cabinet with all of the ice creams inside and I remember getting a cold butt! I thought about my mum telling me when I was a little boy that sitting on the cold surface will give you piles. I couldn't believe that I was thinking this – I never thought about my mum!

Then I started to tell the bloke about God. I told him that I really needed to find a church and that I couldn't get into the churches I had rung locally, because nobody would speak to me in the night-time. So he told me about a Spiritualist place in Paignton. I started to get really excited again and I rushed back to my bedsit to get ready for 'church'.

I put some water in a bowl and I splashed it about a bit. I had no other clothes with me so I couldn't get changed. I left the bedsit again and directly outside a taxi was waiting at the crossroads. I jumped straight into it. Only it wasn't empty and the driver shouted, 'Oi, what are you doing?' In the back was an elderly lady.

I said, 'I'm sorry, but I really need this cab. Wherever she's going I'll pay the fare.' I was desperate, but I had never done anything like that in my life – offer to pay for someone else!

He dropped her off and I said to him, 'My name is Steve Amos.'

'All right,' he said, clearly thinking I was a nutter.

'No, no,' I said. 'My name is Steve Amos, remember it, Steve Amos.'

I was trying to tell him my whole story, but he must have really put his foot down because we were there in absolutely no time at all. He dropped me off right outside the centre and it wasn't open. I was devastated. I hung around outside waiting for it to open until about nine o'clock in the morning. But nothing happened. There was no address and no phone number and no board. I crossed the road to the newsagent's and the shopkeeper told me where the Spiritualist leader lived. So I knocked on his door and a lovely lady answered the door. I said to her, 'I want to speak to your husband.'

'Why?' she asked.

'Because I need to get into that building,' I said, pointing in the direction of the place.

'Oh no,' she said. 'I'm sorry but we're not opening today. We're waiting for another leader to arrive because my husband is very ill.'

I was gutted. I had been trying to get into all of the churches, and I couldn't even get into a

Spiritualist one. I started to believe that nobody wanted me – that it wasn't real. I decided to go back home.

I started walking back up through Preston and I passed Preston Baptist church. I looked up at it and it was massive. It was the sort of church that I used to steal from. I was stood outside thinking that I probably couldn't go into a church anyway because of my past. I wandered around outside thinking that if they saw a shifty looking bloke wandering around, they might come out and say 'Can I help you?' or something. But again nothing happened.

Around the back of the church I found a path that led to the manse. Just as the knocker hit the door, a lady answered with a great big smile on her face. Before I could say a word she had me sat in the kitchen with a cup of tea in my hand. Her name was Betty Quinn. (Thank you Betty!) As I started to try to tell her my story I became excited all over again. I was saying, 'I really need to speak to your husband.'

'I'm sorry but you can't', she said. 'He is really ill up in bed with the 'flu.'

I couldn't believe it. Were there any healthy people in this town?

'I need to go to church,' I said.

She smiled at me, 'I think you might find you're a bit too lively for our congregation. But I do know of a church that has just opened called Living Waters Pentecostal Church.'

I thought, I'm from London, I can do black gospel, Hallelujah! Praise God! Wow! Yeah! Cool!

When she said Pentecostal I read black gospel. I didn't have a clue what it meant! Anyway, she rang Pastor Cliff Tite and arranged for me to meet him outside the church. It happened to be the church opening day – it had just been rebuilt and this was the first day it was open for business.

Not long after Betty's help, I was sat in Cliff's car outside the church chatting with him. I told him about all the 'weird' things that were going on in my life. He didn't have a collar on or anything, which I thought was strange; he was just wearing a jacket and tie. He started to ask me questions.

'When did this happen?'

'Three o'clock this morning,' I replied.

He looked very shocked.

All the time we had been talking I had been watching people going into the church, they were all dressed nice and smart. Pastor Cliff asked me inside.

At the time I didn't know anything about communion services and gospel services and that sort of stuff. All I knew was suddenly I was going in.

The place was full. It must have seated 250 people at least. My main fear was that as I walked in, the entire congregation would turn

and look at me. I really stank of cigarettes and
everything.

That was one interesting thing. God took
away all my cravings for the drugs and stuff,
but I still was smoking. It wasn't for three or
four weeks (when I had learned more about
God) that I kicked the last habit.

I had been entirely unable to handle the hard
drugs and so God dealt with that on my behalf.
I soon found out that I could handle quitting
smoking in partnership with God. It took us
about three weeks and a box and a half of extra
strong mints, but I did kick it!

Anyway, I sat myself down at the back of the
church and I could smell perfume. It was especially wonderful, as I hadn't smelt anything
properly for ten years. I knew what incense or
cannabis smelt like, but I wasn't familiar with
anything normal. My sinuses were shot to
pieces, and as for my taste buds – no way! But
here I was smelling a lady's perfume.

Pastor Cliff stood up at the front and he told
everyone that there was a visitor amongst them
this morning. I thought that at that moment
everybody would turn round and stare – but
nobody did. I was sat on a chair, rocking like
people do when they are nervous, when Cliff
announced that he was going to preach a
gospel message. He preached on John, chapter
3 verse 16, and all about Jesus dying on the
cross. As he talked, I started to wonder whether

or not this was for me. Was this what I was looking for? How much was it going to cost me?

As this thought went through my head, coincidentally, the collection went round and I thought, 'I knew it!' I knew this was going to cost me! I put the last bit of money I had on me into the collection.

I looked round and thought, 'It's all right for this lot, but they've got no idea what my life's been like.' When I had been talking to Pastor Cliff, I had only told him about what had happened to me, I hadn't told him any of the stuff about prison and that.

But he stood and preached – he was addressing everyone but it seemed like he was talking to me – and he appeared amazingly to have an answer for every thought I had. It was as if he was reading my mind. He was talking about two thieves on the cross. I got the impression that it was aimed right at my level. I was being told that it did not matter what I had done, how bad I had been, no matter what anyone else thinks of you, Jesus loves you and God thinks about you. God wants you to go to heaven. And the only way you can go to heaven is through Jesus, God's Son, who died on the cross.

I had, by this stage, become so nervous that I was grabbing tightly onto the chair because it all sounded so good. I had never heard any of this before and it was just what I needed.

When I had been in the car with Pastor Cliff we were talking about God. I had an inside awareness of God. It didn't come to me from outside people talking, but the love-experience was making me aware of certain things, like the world being God's world and how Jesus was coming back. But until this point I had never even heard of Jesus being a real person. I didn't know anything about him, but all of a sudden it made sense – Father, Son and Holy Ghost. Jesus is the Son!

I had always wanted to find a way out at bad points, a way to escape myself. It was going to happen. I was getting even more excited and my heart was racing.

Cliff carried on preaching this incredible message and said, 'If you want to be sure that Jesus is in your life, if you want to be a born-again Christian, if you want everything you've done forgiven – *everything*, no matter how bad, and I mean that, no matter how bad, I want you to come to the front now, and we will pray with you.'

But my fingers were held onto the chair so tightly. I closed my eyes and realised I was going nowhere! 'I'm going nowhere! I'm going nowhere!' But when I opened my eyes (and I've no idea how I got there) I was standing right at the front of the church ready to be prayed with.

I looked around at 250 people who were trying not to notice my bum sticking out of my ripped jeans! They were all shouting 'Hallelujah' and 'Amen' like Pentecostal people do. And I was thinking 'Wow! My bum's out of my jeans and they're shouting "Hallelujah"!'

Pastor Cliff prayed with me.

That was 28th February 1993.

My life totally changed.

I asked Jesus to forgive me and I had a lot to be forgiven for – all the people I had hurt in the past, friends and family. I definitely wanted Jesus in my life so I asked him into my heart. There was no comparison.

13

Everything Is New

The same day I asked Jesus to be involved in my life, I sat down with a man called Dave and he gave me a little red Bible, which contained the New Testament and the Book of Psalms. When he gave it to me I had no idea what to do with it. I couldn't read, I was uneducated and I was told in prison that I was dyslexic. I had tried to read before but had to give up because it could take up to an hour to read just a little, so I couldn't see the point in giving me a book. But I opened it anyway and had quite a surprise. I could read clearly.

I remember in the car with Cliff, when it dawned on me that I was going to be mocked by all the old crowd. I knew that people were really going to have a go at me over what was happening. And I even found it in the Bible that Dave gave to me. Jesus said, 'If the world hates you, remember it hated me first' (John's gospel, chapter 15, verse 18). I looked at these words and they all seemed to come together on the page. It was as if all the letters fell into place and the sentence made sense to me. It was really exciting. I turned around to everyone and said, 'I can read!'

Well – they were excited enough about me coming off the drugs, because their church had been praying for drug addicts and dealers to get to know the gospel and get their lives put back together properly. And they were seeing something that they had prayed for.

And for a minute, I didn't seem that bothered about the drugs miracle – it was nothing in comparison to the discovery that I could read.

This Bible was incredible. I came home from church feeling completely different, and all because I read some amazing things – and they all made sense to me. I was high, but not on drugs, on the love of God. When I got home I sat down with my Bible and I read for ages.

The next day, I went along to the Monday church meeting, and then I went to their Tuesday house group, and then I went to their Wednesday meeting. It was all really cool.

I got myself another Bible with the Old *and* New Testaments in it. I read it from cover to cover in three weeks. I read it all the time. I would get up in the morning and read it, and if there was a meeting happening at the church then I would stop reading to go to it, and then pick up where I left off when I got home. I would go to sleep reading it and then wake up at four o'clock the next morning and start reading again.

It was a very exciting time for me. I was
learning a lot. There were all of these new
things to deal with, like prayer, which I think is
one of the hardest things to explain as a
Christian – the fact that you can talk to somebody who cannot be seen and that it feels good.
It came surprisingly easily, I used to imagine
that God was sitting in a chair and I would just
talk to him. Then I found that wherever I went
I could talk to God because he was always
going to be with me. It was a bit like the way a
child has an imaginary friend. The only difference was I knew God was there. He may well
have been sitting in that chair – although I
know he is everywhere – to me that was
exactly where he was.

Not long after I became a Christian I started
to get up and go for walks on the beach in the
early hours of the morning. I would think about
things that I had never thought about before. I
would watch the waves come in and I would
think how awesome the waves and the water
were. I knew that if the world was flooded
there would be nothing that any of us could do
about it – but that God was in control of even
waves and oceans. I would think about gravity,
about how we are held down on the planet, and
I would look up in wonder at the stars. I was
wondering why I hadn't seen any of this before.
Whenever I had looked at the stars in the past I
had never thought of God, then all of a sudden

I had read in the Bible that God had made the stars, that he knows how many there are, that he knows how many hairs there are on my head. I was totally lost in the greatness of God.

One morning I was on my walk and I had my mouth organ with me. I couldn't play it, but I had read in the Bible that everything that we say, we pray, we sing gets taken up by the angels and presented to God in a pure and orderly manner. So I realised that it didn't matter how bad my playing was, the angels would make it all nice and it would be great because God loves me. He'd look down and think, 'That's my boy playing that!' So I started playing my mouth organ and I'm thinking, 'Lord, this may sound terrible now, but by the time it gets to you it's going to be a masterpiece.'

The tide was out and I was walking along the beach and looking up at the sky thinking about how much I loved God. I stopped and took off my shoe. In big letters I wrote 'JESUS IS ALIVE' in the sand. It was massive. Then I carried on my walk down to the harbour and out along the pier where I stopped to have a chat with some fishermen. When I came back along the beach my writing was still there, and right next to it someone had written 'PRAISE GOD'. Suddenly I realised that I was not the only Christian that went out for walks, and who thought like I did.

There was another time when I went for a walk through Torre Abbey Gardens. I had just managed to give up smoking and my sense of smell was returning properly. I must have looked really strange because I was sniffing around everywhere, and when I went into the gardens I could smell the plants. I had not smelt anything properly for a good ten years at least. I picked a flower and I started to smell it. I was so overwhelmed that I started to cry. It was so wonderful, being able to smell again after so long.

During the previous few years, I had been a bit of a loner; I never really talked to anyone outside my immediate circle of friends. Now all of these new experiences were happening to me and I found I was turning into a new person, together with a new life, in a new world that I was only just starting to notice.

I went to the butchers and I told the man there about the flower and about the drugs and about how I had met with God. He told me that he was very happy for me, but he didn't think it would be very good for him. I told him about me smelling for the first time in ages and I ordered half a pound of Cumberland sausages. I had always loved Cumberland sausages. They reminded me of when I was little – my favourite dinner was Cumberland sausages, mash and cold baked beans!

I went back to the bedsit and put on the frying pan and turned on a tape of Christian music. When the sausages got sizzling there was a smell and I got really excited, shouting 'thank you God', because only God could have given me my sense of smell back. I sat down and said grace – I found that very hard to get used to, thanking God for food – and I dolloped on my tomato sauce. I put the sausage in my mouth and I could taste it.

I was stunned. I could taste. I hadn't tasted food for I don't know how long. I was shouting, 'I love you God!' and I was half expecting the bloke next door to come through the wall and kill me.

Being able to taste again was to be a minor downfall. I could remember when food used to taste good, and I knew yogurts were lovely, and so I went out and I bought food. I was less than seven stone when I came out of hospital, and within a year I had made it up to sixteen stone; I just ate and ate and ate! Part of my trouble was the people at church were so nice and they kept inviting me over for dinner, and I didn't know how to say no. There was a time that I was eating three or four dinners a day in my first couple of weeks as a Christian. I was certainly looked after. God had not only given me a new heart and a new mind, but he had given me new friends and 'family'. I was safe.

14

Back To School!

Three or four weeks after I came off drugs, I went on my first assignment with the church. A couple of the girls from the church (sisters Nina and Louise) arranged a meeting with the headmaster of a local school. He invited me in to school to give a lecture on drugs awareness. It was a very important day for me and I wanted to make sure I did it properly. I got advice from people in the church on how I should prepare myself.

One of the pastors, Mike Symmonds, told me that he listed bullet points on a card like headings, to remind him of the key areas that he wants to talk about. Then, if I were to lose my train of thought, I could look down and I would know what I was saying next.

I was very nervous when I arrived at the school. I was taken to a science room where the seating was tiered like in a cinema. There was a small room at the bottom of the slope where I could get ready. When I stepped out of the room, I found 50 or 60 faces staring down at me expectantly and I felt more than a little intimidated!

'Hello... hello everyone', I began, 'My name's Steve Amos and I'm here today to talk to you about drugs awareness.'

I had my piece of paper in my hand, and I was shaking. I felt like they could all see right through me and so I stared at the piece of paper. Quickly I read out the bullet points from the paper. I was so scared.

'I'm sorry', I said. 'I can't do it like this.'

I put down the piece of paper and started again. I told them my life story and about the drugs, the same way I have told everyone since. I wasn't lecturing, I was just talking to people about what I had learned. It was a good session, and it led to other good sessions. Word spread and I developed the courage to talk to people and crowds.

There was a time when I would practise preaching on the bus from Paignton to Preston. It was a half-hour journey and the benefit for the preacher is, people can't walk away so easily on a bus.

One day I had had a good session in the school. I am only allowed to talk about drugs in the lessons, but during break this particular day, the pupils had asked me how I stopped doing drugs and then I was able to talk about God as well. I got on the bus to go home and suddenly I noticed the difference in atmosphere, from the

laughing and joking of the classroom to the
misery and pain of the lives of the people on the
bus. It upset me and so I started to pray. I
prayed to God to bless the bus (not knowing
whether or not a bus could be blessed!). I knew
God wanted people to be happy and within five
minute the atmosphere on the bus changed.
People had started to talk to each other and we
were all noticeably lifted. I was totally blown
away by the power of praying. This was when I
really knew that prayer worked.

It was at this time that I started to do some
Bible study. I had never studied anything
before, and it was a bit of a shock to the system.
I had my Bible and I went to see a friend of
mine called Doug. Knowing that I was doing a
Bible study, he let me borrow a book. When I
saw it, it was one of the thickest books I had
ever seen. I thought it must have millions
words in it. I didn't realise that it was a com-
panion to the Bible, which *explained* the scrip-
ture. I thought that I was going to have to read
it from cover to cover. So I took it with good
grace, stuck it under my arm and left wondering how on earth I was ever going to finish it.

I had loads of scrap paper, and so I began my
study of the Bible, in particular The power of
the name of Jesus. I used a cross-reference Bible
and found myself getting more and more
excited by what I was learning. I was finding
the Bible was more complete than I had ever

previously imagined. For example, I started to find references to Jesus in the Old Testament – and I realised that God really had a plan for the whole earth. Jesus' death was no accident. God had sent him to die on purpose, so that he could have people like me in Heaven with him, for all eternity. This was so cool! God actively looked for me, to save me. I realised I hadn't slept for three days, so I went to see Pastor Mike and started to tell him about how excited I was.

'Do you realise just how much power there is in the name of Jesus?' I asked him. He was so patient with me! Here I was learning something new – and he had known it for ages. But even still, I think he shared my excitement.

As we talked, it was obvious he was pleased for me, but he realised I hadn't slept for a few days, and he tried to convince me to rest a bit.

But I didn't want to rest and so I went to a Christian bookshop in Paignton and asked in there if they had any books on the power of the name of Jesus. I had no idea what an incredibly wide subject it was.

'Yes sir, nearly every book you see here is about the power of the name of Jesus.'

'No,' I said, 'specifically on the power of the name of Jesus.'

And so they found for me a book called *In The Name Of Jesus*.

I didn't really want to read books, but I thought I ought to as I was doing some study.

The book talked about the miracles Jesus did while he walked the earth. It also talked about the Devil and the limited authority he has to try and do bad things.

After reading it, I felt like I could do anything. After all, if the Bible said it, I simply believed it. I was convinced that all I needed was the power of the name of Jesus. I was dead right!

15

The Power Of the Name

My first experience of spiritual warfare, of going out into the world and doing what Jesus did, came in the form of praying for troubled and sick people. It came about as the result of an article in the local newspaper, the *Herald Express*, all about my going into schools to talk about my life. In school I was only allowed to talk about the drugs side of my life – unless I was specifically asked why I stopped taking drugs – but this article stated that I was willing to talk to anyone about any aspect of my life, whether it be the drugs or whether it be my new-found life with God. People could contact the paper, who would let my church know that someone wanted to talk to me for advice.

I received a telephone call from a lady named Doreen. She told me that she was a member of the Salvation Army. I thought that this sounded really cool, but as ever, I had no idea what this actually was. Then I asked her if she was a born-again Christian and she told me she was. Her being a born-again Christian made it easier for me to understand. In conversation we talked about many things, but she started to tell me about friends of hers – an elderly couple, Ethel and Bert, who lived in a bungalow in Paignton. She told me that, at night, when they were in bed, things would move across the room and they felt like they were being touched by an outside 'presence'. This story reminded me of my spiritualism days when I felt myself pinned to the bed and I knew just how scary it could be. As she told me more and more about it I started to think, 'in the name of Jesus I can deal with this'.

'Would it be all right for me to arrange for you to see them?' she asked.

'Yeah!' I said, thinking that this was my first chance to make a difference.

On the day we arranged to see them, Doreen came out of her house carrying a Bible in one hand and a cross in the other. I used to watch the old horror films about exorcisms and that sort of stuff, and looking at her made me want to laugh out loud – not in a nasty way, but because of what I had read. I was thinking that it had nothing to do with carrying a big book or a big emblem of a cross, but that it was entirely the power of the name of Jesus – the power that came from the cross and the power that comes from believing in God's word.

I didn't realise at the time that Doreen maybe felt stirred up in faith to do great things if she carried around her biggest Bible and her favourite cross. I was still young as a Christian and there were still gaps in my understanding of people. But I do think God was interested in seeing how far I was prepared to believe that Jesus was the answer to every problem.

When we arrived at the bungalow, I knocked on the door and I suddenly felt incredibly deflated. I didn't have a clue why; it was the first major sign of depression since I had found God. It unnerved me a bit, but I made an active choice to ignore it. Good job too.

'Hello,' said Ethel, answering the door. 'Come on in. I've just put the kettle on so we can have a nice cup of tea.'

Doreen introduced me and we sat down in the living room where I met Bert sitting in his chair. Their cat came in and sat down next to me. The couple were surprised; 'The cat is never friendly to anyone who comes here.'

I was not really very surprised. I simply assumed that because God made the animals, the animals would know God. It was like the cat could sense that I knew God, and so it was happy to sit with me!

We started to talk about the problems they were having.

Ethel explained, 'I can be stood in the kitchen, and it feels like someone has come up behind me. But when I turn around there's nobody there.'

'This is no problem,' I said, with an air of confidence. 'I can go and deal with this for you now, just show me your bedroom.' Somehow I knew that this was the place to start.

As I walked through the door it slammed shut behind me. *Bang!* I jumped a mile. I panicked as the wardrobe doors swung open and closed on their hinges. I was so shocked with the activity that was obviously coming from an unseen personality that I didn't know what to do. I felt helpless. Funnily, I'd just finished a three-day study looking at the Bible's references to the awesome power in the name of Jesus, but here I was, feeling quite helpless. But, as I made my way to the door, suddenly I started to feel the power of the name of Jesus flow through my body. And I started to demonstrate the confidence, authority and purity of Jesus' name. My arm lifted up into the air and I started to speak aloud, praising God.

I walked through the bungalow praying aloud. I went into all the rooms praying: the toilet, the bathroom, the kitchen, the closets, and every little room. The confidence was amazing. At the time I didn't have a clue why I was doing what I was doing, but I knew that it was combating the plans of the devil for these people's lives.

The Bible says that the thief (the Devil) only comes to steal, kill or destroy (John's gospel, chapter 10, verse 10). In other words, when he affects our lives, it is only ever negative or destructive. When God, on the other hand, has a plan for our lives, it is to give us hope and a future (Jeremiah, chapter 29, verse 11).

When I felt it was over I went back into the living room.

'God is wonderful,' Ethel said.

'I hope I didn't scare you,' I said.

'Oh no,' she replied. 'When you speak like that we know that it is God moving.'

'Here you go, son, sit down,' said Bert, standing up and offering me his chair.

'He's never done that!' said Ethel, explaining that Bert was very protective of 'his' chair. I had gained his approval!

The elderly couple had recognised what I was doing as speaking in tongues (Acts, chapter 2). It turned out that they both used to go to a Pentecostal church before they moved to Torbay. Since they had moved into the area, because they were sick, they had not established a habit of going to church.

I told them about what had happened in the bedroom with the wardrobe and the power of God, and that I was convinced any problems were now gone through the power in his name.

As we talked more I learned that Bert was diabetic and Ethel was epileptic. Doreen suggested that we pray for them concerning their sicknesses. I thought about what I had read in the Bible.

'When was the last time you went to church?' I asked them.

'I'd say about nine years ago,' Ethel told me. Bert nodded in agreement.

'Do you understand that if you leave God and want to return to him then you must repent of your sins. In nine years you must have done things that were wrong, but if you pray for forgiveness now, ask Jesus back into your life, I can pray for you and your sickness will go.'

I must have sounded like a book, but that was because everything I had learnt was largely out of a book – the Bible. Doreen was looking at me encouragingly. This surprised me, since she was the more experienced Christian, but the couple obviously found it easy to understand me, and so we prayed.

Knowing their lack of transport, I asked them, if I could arrange it, would they be interested in coming to church the next day. They said they would and I phoned my pastor, Mike, there and then.

'Can you send someone down to give them a lift?'

And so it was sorted. We agreed that I would meet them at the church entrance before the service. They thanked us again and Doreen and I left.

Meanwhile, that evening I called in to see a young lad, a friend of a friend. I stayed with him a long time, and arranged to see him the following morning before I went to church. When we met the next morning our conversation went on and I lost track of time. I had promised to meet Ethel and Bert at the door, but I was too late, and by the time I arrived the service had already started.

Looking around the room I couldn't see them. I started to think that they might have left because I had failed to be there for them. I began to cry.

At this time I was sitting at the front row in every service. This particular morning, I sat with my eyes tight shut. All through the meeting I was saying, 'I'm sorry God, I'm so sorry, I'm really sorry.'

I heard the pastor say, 'If any of you have illnesses, or if you've recently re-dedicated your life to Jesus, I want you to come forward and I will to pray for you.'

This made me feel worse because I blamed myself for the couple not being there. Then I opened my eyes. Stood directly in front of me were Ethel and Bert. They were at the front of the church and they were holding hands. It was awesome! I had learnt another great lesson.

When I went home to the bedsit I prayed. Pacing the room, as I did when I prayed, I told God how I realised my shortcomings and that I should take time to learn about people. I was not to try to solve all of the world's problems, but to submit to God's timing for his purposes in my life.

But many times since then, I have been in similar circumstances. My nature is to be involved with people and to help. The Bible indicates that where our own abilities end, God takes over, and very often it's when we're totally out of our own depth that the intervening of the power of God makes the difference.

Clearly the Christian life was, and is, meant to be an adventure. And I think that the minute we have learned it all is the minute we are taken to be with God – translated from one life to the next. The only thing we can be sure of is that nothing stays the same. Life is for learning!

Coda

And so we come to the point in my story where we find a natural conclusion. I have learnt an important lesson, that life as a Christian was still only just beginning for me, and I still have a lot to learn. My lecturing in schools went from strength to strength. Soon I fell in love with a young lady from the church. Her name was Nanette and we were married on Friday, 13 August 1993. I have since travelled across the United States, speaking about what God has done in my life. Many, many people in England and abroad have been delivered from the hold of drugs and from lifestyles that were slowly killing them, being 'set free' by the power of God.

I try to talk simply, in language that normal people understand, about the relevance of the Bible today. It contains the power of God to transform lives. And all the time I see people who cry out to God for help being helped, because what God does for one, he will do for another. He doesn't have any favourites, and you don't have to go out of your way to please him so you can get your miracle. God just loves to put peoples' lives back together again!

Nanette and I have two sons, Freddie and Dudley, and I am learning once again the skills required to be a good father. I have even been in contact with my own mum and dad.

I may not know what the future has in store for me, but I know that I have Jesus to thank for my having survived the abuse I put myself through, and for that I shall be eternally thankful.

This is just the beginning for me – and it can be for you too. You know, if Jesus did it for me, then I know he can do it for you; he really can set you free.

I tried very hard to say how sorry I was to Heidi. I tried to tell Marie, who was three years old, what had happened to her daddy and that Jesus had made him better. I said I was sorry and she simply said, 'Thank you Jesus for helping my daddy'. I have not seen her or Heidi since then. I've tried to trace Marie's whereabouts many times, but I know one day – probably out of the blue – she'll call on me and be able to meet her new brothers, Freddie and Dudley.

I hope you have enjoyed this simple account of my life. I pray for you, the reader of this book, that you will find what is missing in your life and be brave enough to do something about it.

A little prayer

> I admit Lord Jesus, that I am a sinner
>   and I want you to forgive my sins
> I know that it is your will to make me a new
>   person, even on the inside
> Come and live in me Lord Jesus by Your Holy
>   Spirit and put Your love in my heart.
> I want you to take away all the bad memories and
>   habits, that I can't cope with anymore.
> I need your help to make a new start
> Thank you Lord Jesus that your death on the
>   cross has made all this possible
> Amen

If you have prayed this prayer for the first time in your life, you really need to tell someone.

In the town where you live, find out where a Bible-believing church is. This can either be a Gospel Hall, a Baptist church, Methodist or Pentecostal church to name but a few. There are many vicars or pastors who can offer you advice and help, just like they did for me.

You'll know their advice is right, if it comes from the Bible.

You will also need to get yourself a Bible as soon as possible. There are some very easy to understand versions about, like the Good News Bible for instance, which talk in normal English, about the life of Jesus.

God bless you in your new life!